The Lady of all Nations
Who Once was Mary

The Lady of all Nations Who Once was Mary:

Co-Redemptrix, Mediatrix, Advocate

Peter Klos, S.S.S.

Queenship

PUBLISHING COMPANY
P.O. Box 42028 Santa Barbara, CA 93140-2028
(800) 647-9882 • (805) 957-4893 • Fax: (805) 957-1631

DEDICATION

I first of all dedicate this book to Mary, Co-Redemptrix, Mediatrix, and Advocate. Further, I dedicate it to all women who through their lives have made Mary present in the world. I mention Mrs. Th. Thomas and Joyce Miranda; without their love for Jesus this book would not have been realized.

On October 14, 1966, Pope Paul VI approved a Decree of the Congregation of Doctrine, which declared that it was permissible to publish all apparitions, miracles and revelations of supernatural nature without an "Imprimatur" of the Church authorities.

As author of this book, I'd very much like to declare that, for me personally, all the private revelations discussed in this book are of divine origin. Nevertheless, I subject myself in advance to the judgement of the Church regarding all apparitions and revelations which are discussed in this book and about which the Church has not yet given a definite judgement.

This book has only one purpose, namely to clarify the importance of certain revelations, to explain the "logic" of them in order to contribute to the realization of God's Salvation plan for mankind.

© 1998 Queenship Publishing

Library of Congress #: 97-75825

Published by:
Queenship Publishing
P.O. Box 42028
Santa Barbara, CA 93140-2028
(800) 647-9882 • (805) 957-4893 • Fax: (805) 957-1631

Printed in the United States of America

ISBN: 1-57918-049-3

CONTENTS

TRANSLATOR'S NOTES

The author's book: *The Lady of All Nations Who Once was Mary: Co-Redemptrix, Mediatrix and Advocate*, which discuss what might soon be declared the last Dogma about Her, has thrilled and even moved me in many parts as it was new knowledge to me. However, translating the book does not always mean that I have to agree with the opinions of the author or quotations of the visionaries, as in the case of Vassula Ryden, who has been rejected recently by the "Teaching of the Church."

As there are many "ups and downs" in the Netherlands, as well as in the English-speaking countries within our Catholic Church, there is all the more reason to keep close to the "Teaching of the Church" and not to foster more "ups and downs" and confusion in relation to the author's subjection to the Church's judgement. For this reason, the question above is still under discussion and consideration with *Vox Populi Dei* in English-speaking countries, while the book is being printed.

The translation would not have taken place for several reasons: Firstly, if out of love and devotion to Mother Mary I did not want to help in promoting the coming new Dogma as a sign of my loyalty to Her. Secondly, if Brendan Hegarty, S.F.O. would not have helped me so generously in the text proof and on the computer, of which I am a Year One student.

This translation would not yet have seen the light of day. Hence, *Deo gratias ad maiorem Dei gloriam*, Thanks be to God, Who created Mother Mary for our salvation.

Fr. Dirk Tolboom, M.H.M.

Lord Jesus Christ, Son of the Father,
send now Your Spirit over the earth.
Let the Holy Spirit live in the hearts of all Nations,
that they may be preserved from degeneration,
disaster and war.
May the Lady of All Nations,
who once was Mary,
be our Advocate!
Amen.

FOREWORD

Mary, with this name I would like to start this book. Mary, a name that calls forth all that is most beautiful in the human being. A name that gives consolation and has given it to numerous people in need. A name which was on the lips of many people in the hour of their death. A name which gives confidence and enables people to trust themselves to the darkness of the unknown.

Mary, the name with the most beautiful sound in the history of mankind.

Till Easter 1992, Mary did not play an important role in the witnessing of my faith. She was always there, no doubt. I never even doubted her greatness. Since I was about twenty-five years of age, I have very deeply understood that she is the Mother of God. This insight was enough for me never to have any trace of doubt about her importance in God's plan of salvation for mankind. But yet, Mary was hardly emphatically present. I was totally tuned towards Jesus: He was — and is — my God and Lord and with His words I was content. I never even went to Mary's pilgrim's places. Once I was on holiday in Lourdes and visited the grotto there, but I never felt a need to go especially to a pilgrimage place of Mary to meet her there. In Lourdes I saw the film about Bernadette. What struck me most in the film was the episode from the life of Bernadette as a nun. When her Superior thought to give Bernadette a favor by offering her a journey to Lourdes to obtain a healing from the growth in her knee, Bernadette said, somewhat astonishingly, "But Lourdes is not for me." The same feeling I also experienced. I had nothing against Lourdes or other places of pilgrimage, but I never had the idea that Mary had something to say to me there. I believed in the Gospel already and whatever I needed I could find in the Gospel.

From Easter 1992 onwards, many things have happened in my life. It has been Mary herself, who from that time onwards has led me to understand the meaning of her apparitions. Also, she has let me see something of her power and beauty and of her place in God's plan of salvation. She has let me see especially which part she at present performs in the time in which we live. It is an enormous privilege, which has been given to me to get to know Mary like this. It is a privilege because I would never had understood the greatness and especially the love of Mary so deeply if Mary herself had not shown me this. This election was accompanied with the unlimited fury of Satan. What I especially have understood from Mary is that she indeed is the woman who crushes the head of the serpent as it is described in the Book of Revelation. When Mary attracted me to herself, it looked at a certain moment as if hell had exploded above me. In a very short time I had to lose everything that was dear to me. With many people I fell out of grace and lost the confidence of many with whom I had lived for many years. Suspicion, slander and disapprovals became my lot. Yet, I was never worried. It was something that overcame me and that very clearly came "from Heaven," so that I have never lost the peace from my heart and have always had the certainty that everything and everyone whom I had to lose, would return to me again. That finally everything would cooperate with the plans of Mary, which aim towards the happiness — the true happiness — of all people.

Also, the writing of this book has, according to my experience and conviction been an inspiration of Mary herself. It was an unspeakable joy to work at it. Through reading and writing about Mary, I understood ever better and deeper who she is. Sometimes I would already experience something of what Jesus says to Maria Valtorta in a revelation: "To have only a glimpse of Mary means blessedness. The eternal blessedness consists in the contemplation of God. Mary is a kind of a clear window towards God, so that whoever sees her, sees God."

The book is written, as it states in the introduction, to support the last Marian Dogma. I hope that it is not the theological power of conviction in the first place that may touch the reader, but much more the beauty and love of Mary. It is the beauty and love of Mary that can purify our soul from all darkness and evil.

May this book be a contribution to the way mankind has to go, in order to come via the Mother to the Son and, thus, find the way to God, the Holy Trinity, for whom all things live.

Amsterdam, 8 December, 1993
Feast of Mary's Immaculate Conception

Peter Klos, S.S.S.

INTRODUCTION

This book is meant to be a support of the last Marian Dogma, which will be explained by the Church. The Dogma will explain that Mary may be known as Coredemptrix, Mediatrix of all graces and Advocate for the People of God. The announcement of this last Dogma about Mary we can find in the messages of "The Lady of All Nations" received in Amsterdam.

A Dogma is an indisputable doctrine about a definite aspect of the Catholic Faith. When a Dogma is proclaimed, it then belongs to the inheritance of the Catholic Faith itself and is valid for all centuries. The Dogmas, which the Church has so far proclaimed about Mary, are concerned with Her Immaculate Conception, Her permanent Virginity, Her Motherhood of God and Her Assumption into Heaven. These are all Dogmas which say something about the historical existence of Mary of Nazareth; about the special graces which God has given Her in Her existence. This last Dogma is concerned with the glorified Mary (with "the Lady of all Nations, who once was Mary") and deals with the power, which God has given Her and with the place which She occupies in God's actual acts of Redemption. It deals with Mary in Heaven, and Her significance for the Church on earth.

A Dogma is a theological verbal expression of a mystery of Faith. Therefore, Dogmas ask for a theological accountability and explanation. Yet, this is not a theological book in the ordinary sense of the word. It has been written for learned and for ordinary faithful. Perhaps mostly for the last group, because they generally have more faith than the learned. It is no theological book in the ordinary sense of the word, because it is not written according to ordinary theological methods. This has been done with an unavoidable purpose: the present day theology with her methods and criteria is in principle inadequate to comprise a mystery as is contained in the Dogma. The present day theology is poisoned by rationalism which makes it to a certain extent incompetent to realize its own objectives. The aim of theology is, of course, to clarify the faith and to interpret the revelation of God. Rationalism cannot only start from a predetermined faith or a predetermined revelation. In rationalism only that is true which is measurable and can be verified with a limited mind. To illustrate this I will tell you of a small experience which I had in the preparation of this book. In a theological bookshop I was looking for a book by Prof. Schillebeeck and Prof. Halker about Mary. I found it immediately; there was a big pile of them. I looked a bit further and asked a saleswoman if there were books with texts about Mary which were a bit more traditional, such as Bernardus or Grignion de Monfort. First, she looked at me a bit puzzled but then she directed me to a small shelf where, as she said, there were still some pious booklets. On this shelf I found many pearls from the Catholic tradition: Fathers of the Church, Saints, Mystics. Many of these editions were made by the Abbey of Bonheiden. But there were, also, still other precious booklets and various books for which there is almost no interest. No doubt this book will meet the same fate by many "learned," if they take the trouble to read it, it will be put aside as non-scientific or in the best case as "pious literature." Let it be so; on the other hand, it will be understood by the simple of heart, by people who can listen to their heart, whether they are learned or not.

In a scientific book, it is important to mention the sources and indicate exactly where in which book and on which page the quotation or reference can be found again. This book will have nothing to do with this method. In the first place, it is a lot of useless work. My own experience is — I have studied at three universities — that nobody really checks the references and secondly, it is a matter of the content and not the packing. Every kindly disposed reader can trace that my sources are trustworthy and that the spirit of tradition is preferred to the literal quotations. We can approach the book in the spirit of faith. As rationalism is fundamentally insufficient in understanding the divine mysteries, so is a rational critical attitude fundamentally incapable to understand the contents of this book. Rationalism is for the faith a greater evil than sin itself. The sin can be forgiven by a visible sorrow, whilst rationalism in principle shuts off the way to God's offer of love, to His pardon and cuts off the way to the understanding of His mysteries.

In this introduction I do not mind to mention the sources of this book. The first and most important source is the Holy Spirit Himself Who showed me something of the greatness and place of Mary in God's salvific plan. The Holy Spirit worked in many people in the past and still does so today. Such instruments of God, who shed much light on the subject, which is discussed in this book are eg. the prophets of the Old Testament; the evangelists and the writers of the Catholic letters. Further, the Fathers of the Church and the saints, such as Bernardus, Grignion de Montfort, Augustine, John of the Cross, and Theresa of Lisieux. In our times, also, the prophets and instruments of the Holy Spirit such as: Adriane of Speyer, Marthe Robin, Chiara Lubich, Maria Valtorta, Vasula Ryden, Mother Teresa, the visionaries of Fatima, Garabandal, Medjugorje, A.C. Emmerich, Don Gobbi, Mgr. Michelini, Frank Duff and many more. These are all people whom God uses and still does use to make known His intentions with the world and mankind. I have drunk from these sources; I have not approached them with a critical rational mind, but with a simple spirit of faith. I have refreshed myself with them as a baby does with the mother's milk. And although I was not "critical" (in the scientific sense of the word), it has given me the intuitive certainty of the Good, Truth and Beauty.

The booklet of Prof. Schillebeeck and Prof. Halkes is an example of the way in which many theologians think and speak about Mary. They really are a trend for a great (I do not say "important") pattern in today's theology. Prof. Schillebeeck represents the modern systematic theology and Prof. Halkes represents feminism. The anxiety of the modern theologians is that Mary is placed too centrally. This anxiety is justified through the thesis that the true Mariology should be based on the Bible and that Mary may not darken the view of Christ Who really is the end. To start with the second argument: it is evident that everything is ultimately directed towards Christ. This does not only apply to Mary but to the whole of creation. Jesus is the Alpha and Omega; for Him every knee shall bend. He is the incarnate Word of God, the Redeemer and Saviour.

The Incarnation is the mystery of mysteries, as Father Korse so well sings of in his book, *Farewell Christianity* and around this Christ mystery everything in Christianity is turning. Whoever thinks that Mary could ever compete with Jesus, has understood not only nothing of tradition, but has also understood still nothing of Jesus. "Whoever does not honour My Mother, does not need to come also to Me," says Jesus to Maria Valtorta. It is clear that everything that has been said about Mary and still is said, has as the ultimate purpose to know and understand Christ better. But with this not everything has been said. The reverse is namely also the case. The better we understand Mary, Her greatness and Her place in the salvific plan of God, the better we also understand Christ and — if it is good — the more we begin loving Him. Mary is the instrument, which God uses to bring people to Christ (Mary Mediatrix) and the better we understand the instrument, the quicker and more effectively we come to Jesus. Mary has no single self-interest: Her only desire is to teach people the love for Her Son (Mary Immaculate Conception — She is without concupiscence and only conceived by the Holy Spirit). (Mary always Virgin — She is the Mother only concerned for Her Son and who knows the purpose of Her Son for mankind). (Mary, Mother of God) From all eternity Mary was destined to receive the Word of God and to be with soul and body one with that Word. Hence, Mary is soul and body assumed into Heaven. All dogmas about Mary, as She says in the messages of Amsterdam, had to come first in order to understand more deeply the meaning of the Dogma of Mary being Co-redemptrix, Mediatrix and Advocate.

Also, the argument of the biblical foundation is clear. With the New Testament the Revelation has to come to an end; in principle everything has been said, what God wanted to tell mankind. But this does not exclude a progressive revelation, an ongoing better understanding of the Good News of the Bible. Our present private revelations and apparitions do certainly not give any new details about this Revelation of the Bible. They only clarify certain details and pronouncements. In the Bible everything has been in principle said about Mary, be it in a nutshell. The later Tradition has under the power and guidance of the Holy Spirit understood better, what certain texts eg. "The Lady" meant and that these texts were related to Mary.

Prof. Schillebeeck in his booklet opposes these two pronouncements from Tradition, viz. *Never enough about Mary* and *Jesus is the solution of all problems.* He denies the truth of these pronouncements and finds this a bit too much of the good and a projection of all human frustrations and desires. This is one of the most clear signs that Prof. Schillebeeck has little understanding of the spirit of the Tradition... Quite understandably, if we consider his rationalistic starting points. For a rationalist neither Mary nor Jesus is the solution of all problems. For the simple reason, because the rational truth is only a very superficial aspect of the human reality. Neither Jesus nor Mary respond to the many rational questions which man can put. But the truth is not merely rational; The truth is far more relational. And in this relational level Jesus is certainly the solution of all problems and we can never praise Mary enough. Jesus gives purpose and meaning to everything in the life of a believing person. He is the soul of the soul of the person who has surrendered his or her life to God. He makes the deepest darkness light and gives peace and even joy in the most bitter suffering. Jesus is God and as such the meaning of the whole life of the faithful, even if he cannot give a straight answer to all small-minded questions of the intellect.

It is exactly this relational sense which is lacking with Prof. Schillebeeck and Prof. Halkes. For feminism — for which I like to see Prof. Halkes as representative — Mary is either a remnant of the Old Mother goddess from pre-Christian religions or a common believing woman. Prof. Halkes, herself, takes a moderate central position and says that Mary "has become very dear to her." But also for her, Mary is no more than an image, indeed an inspiring image for her, but certainly no more than that. Mary is no actual person with whom one can have a relation, as lively as the relation between two loved ones or between a mother and a son or daughter. The feministic outlook on Mary is nothing but banal. To consider Mary as a remnant of the Old Mother-goddess from pre-Christian religions shows an unheard of and total incomprehension for what Mary in reality is, viz. that from all eternity she was elected Mother of God. And to see Mary as an ordinary faithful woman is a bit less banal, but it gives similar evidence of a total incomprehension of the uniqueness and greatness of Mary. Yet this book is not meant to be polemic or controversial against present day trends in theology. It wants not to be polemic, because it is fruitless and in principle impossible to oppose a theology which is based on rationalistic starting points. This book and the rationalistic theology are two levels of understanding, they are two different languages which will never meet each other in eternity. I have only wanted to show this to clarify why this book will not be taken seriously by many contemparies and with what attitude: an attitude of the heart with which this book has to be read in order to be able to receive the light of it.

The Second Vatican Council — where I feel myself as a child — has no special document dedicated to Mary. There were several reasons for this. There was the reason already mentioned: that the Council Fathers — on advice of Prof. Schillebeeck — were afraid, that Mary would draw too much attention and honor and that She would be placed too much in the center instead of Christ. Especially, ecumenical pros and cons were great; before the Reformation certain declarations about Mary would be unacceptable. Pity enough, this is also the case among many of our Catholics of today. But perhaps there was a more important motive to include Mary into the document about the Church, because according to many Council Fathers Mary primarily "belongs at home with the redeemed People of God," thus to the Church. This argument won and the minority of the Council Fathers, who wanted a separate document about Mary had to be satisfied with this.

In the documents of the Second Vatican Council Mary was first of all seen as belonging to the People of God and thus She got a place in the document of "Lumen Gentium," a decree about the Church. In this document Mary is called Co-operator of the Redemption and also an example of the redeemed and called Christian. This is, of course, all true and this book will not diminish this truth. But it is also true, that by this approach, Mary's unique and important place in God's plan of salvation does not come to its full light. The Second Vatican Council — which is, of course, not the end — has regarding Mary to be supplemented in order to make clear just this unique redemptive significance of Mary for mankind. The fact that Mary was first of all proposed as "belonging to the People of God," should not lead to put Her on one and the same level as all the faithful. Mary really differs from all other people, namely in what is laid down in the Dogma of the Immaculate Conception. In relation to Jesus, Mary is in anticipation — what should be now clear to you — already protected from original sin. In advance Mary has received the Redemption of Christ and She has never known the stain of any sin. From all eternity this was God's plan: a creature, a woman, who would be a complete creature. This would mean: She would live in total dependence on God, in total openness to the Word of God; a creature, who would transcend beyond her own limitation by an unlimited and unconditional trust in God; a creature who would be only "YES" in order to neutralise the "NO" of Eve. In this sense Mary is really "one of us," but at the same time different from us. She is different from us in the sense that She had no need of redemption as we have; She had already, in advance, received the redemption. She was different from us in the sense: what has already been realized in Her, will only happen to us really and definitely, once we are in Heaven. In a certain sense, Mary consequently stands opposite to us at the side of Christ. However, the "standing opposite" means a stronger communion with us and a deeper union with us than if she had not been "immaculately conceived!" It is not just to play the Uniqueness of Mary off against us in order to place Her with all power "at our side." It would do injustice to Mary and ultimately destroy the ultimate purpose: viz. by making Mary "just like us" (True, She is indeed the Mother of Jesus, but that does make Her yet different). Mary becomes ultimately less one with us, because original sin exactly keeps us separate from each other, and puts a limit to our mutual love. With this limitation Mary has no problem; She loves us with a unique and an absolute disinterested love. A love to which we all are indeed called but which for us in this earthly life will never be entirely perfect.

The Second Vatican Council was an important happening in our period. We live in a period which is called by Jesus and Mary in many apparitions and private revelations an "end of times." The "end of times" is something different from the end of the world about which the Gospel speaks. The hour of the end of the world is only known to God the Father, as we know from the Gospel. The "end of times," in which we now live, means the end of a period, the end of an epoch, after which a new period will follow. A new period for the Church and the world, in which Mary and the Holy Spirit will play a very central part. The many apparitions and private revelations in our time are really a "sign of the times," as Cardinal Ratzinger also calls them. Jesus and Mary try with all their powers to convince mankind that the world has deteriorated and that only a conversion of heart, a conversion to Christ can prevent "that people get lost for all eternity." The language of the these messages may appear severe and hard. But it is no other language than that which is used in the Gospels. However, it is repugnant to the present day person to talk about Hell and our eternal rejection or condemnation, yet it is undeniably an important part of the "Glad News." As a matter of fact, the whole Bible goes about the eternal destination of man with as final consequences: the eternal happiness of God or the eternal rejection. The modern man prefers not to hear about this, because it widely exceeds his rational patterns and only brings him thus into problems. This also holds good for the reality such as "the ends of times." Though this is a subject which really cannot be denied — the signs are too clear for this — they prefer not to burn their fingers and hesitate to indicate clearly certain signs of our time. Hypocrites, says Jesus you do recognize the direction of the wind and the rising of the sun; why do you not recognize the obvious sign of our time?

This book is about Mary, placed at the end of times, which we may experience. It is especially meant as a song of praise to Mary, Co-redemptrix, Mediatrix and Advocate. It is She to whom the world and mankind — so far as they will be saved — have to be grateful for their salvation.

In the first chapter an outline will be given of our time of the signs, which indicate, that we live in the end of times, so that in the next three chapters we acknowledge Mary, love Her and call upon Her under the threefold title, which is given to Her by God. Under these titles and in this capacity She, together with the Church, will lead the world to the victory of the merciful love of Jesus and Her Immaculate Heart.

May the Lady of all Nations, Who once was Mary be the Advocate with God to beg a very special blessing over this book.

CHAPTER 1

THE END OF TIMES

In many of the messages (of Vassula, Marguerite, Mgr. Michelini, Don Gobbi, Fatima, Amsterdam, Medjugorje, and others) Jesus and Mary speak very clearly about the approaching end, about "the great trial." The end that will coincide with great calamities and horrors, will take place before long. Many messages, already given to Anna Maria Taigi in 1830, speak about the second half of our century, which is very much in the light of the power of evil and will reach its climax before the year 2000. Vasula received the message at the end of the years "80," that the scourge of God will very soon descend over the earth: (very soon is meant according to Jesus in terms of our era). The approaching will occur not only with great catastrophes and horrors but also with unmistakable signs from Heaven, as was promised in Garabandal, Medjugorje and other places. They will be signs which will be visible to everyone and undeniable. Yet, there will be people who in spite of the great evidence of these signs will not convert themselves. It is the mystery of evil: the mystery like the rejection of Jesus by the people during His earthly life, in spite of the evident compassion of His words and works.

The content of the messages is apocalyptic. It is about worldwide, even cosmic events which are awaiting us. When we, for example, look at the messages of Amsterdam, we can't escape that these bring us at least to thinking. The messages were given in the years 1940-1950, in a time when nobody could foresee what the future viz. the second half of our century would bring. They were happenings, not so much as being related to the coming disaster, but such as the prediction of the Second Vatican Council; the death of Pope Pius XII, (happenings which humanly speaking could not be foreseen), certain messages, predictions, which one in the course of time till today sees as becoming truth.

The messages of the "Lady" predict the global exodus of priests and religious after the Council, the fall of Communism, the difficulties round the British Royal Family, the war in Iran, the Balkan war, the chemical warfare — also the unification of Europe was already predicted with the remark that the unification could only succeed in a right spirit, not in a spirit of self-interest. "The Lady" also warns for all kinds of dangerous developments within the Church. And this was predicted at a time, when the Church in the Netherlands was still flourishing and strong and nobody could suspect the deterioration which started from the year "60 onwards." The Lady warns for false dogmas, especially regarding the Eucharist and bad ecumenism. We only need to glance at the situation of the Dutch Church in order to see how true these warnings were. In the messages of Amsterdam many economical disasters were also predicted; Also, regarding this, one does not need to have prophetical gifts to understand today that such economical disasters are practically unavoidable. The same holds good for predicted environmental disasters, also again in a time when the environment was no anxiety for anybody. In my conviction we cannot any longer disregard the many urgent and warning messages which are given to us from Heaven all over the world. It is highly irresponsible to treat these phenomena of no importance with terms as "mass-suggestions" or even as "mass-hysteria." If we believe that the Church is the lasting presence of Christ in history — and the Church has already acknowledged many private revelations, of which Fatima is perhaps the most known — then we have to take these messages seriously and also to take the remedy seriously, which Jesus and Mary offer us. The leaders of the Church should also do this. It is, of course, their responsibility to determine whether the messages are really of divine origin or not. But a too great prudence can turn into fear. And fear is incompatible with the faith (belief) in an all good and all knowing God. Fear cripples man and makes him unfit to preach the Will of God courageously and to fulfil it. Hence, may the leaders of the Church conquer all fear and understand the signs of the time.

We could still further describe which signs of the time indicate the approaching end. These signs are recognizable and distinguishable to everyone whether we believe or not. It is clear to everyone, that we live in a world of aggression, full of corruption, full of confusion. The major part of mankind suffers hunger or lives in situations of war, suppression or dictatorship... Mankind is afflicted by disasters such as AIDS, abortion, euthanasia, unbridled pornography on all levels, even reaching the beastly level with children and animals. Catastrophes of the environment are a frequent happening and also calamities in technical and scientific fields such as: air disasters, accidents with nuclear power stations, disastrous computer mistakes etc., Mankind is unhappy and desperate: most marriages fail; one can hardly talk about sound upbringing of children; countries are flooded with refugees, racism and fanatic nationalism are popping up everywhere and political leaders listen only to the favor of the voters and have lost all moral consciousness etc. The disasters which overflow the western world are plenty and nobody really knows a way out.

Within the Church it is not much different. Regarding the western world there is a growing lethargy among the priests. (On the other side, there are also priests and religious of the "New Age," but they still represent a small minority) The faith — also among priests who are the first responsible — in the Hierarchy, in the Sacraments especially in the Eucharist, in Celibacy and the morality of the Church, is practically gone.

In 1943 Jesus gave to Maria Valtorta a message about the end of times. It was war and at that moment there were horrible things happening in Italy and the rest of Europe. And yet Jesus predicted that these horrors were only a small storm in comparison with the hurricane which will come over the world. In reality we can only acknowledge that the gale of World War II has meanwhile reached hurricane force: catastrophes and misery have come down on the world and Church and who knows what is still coming. All these signs are, however, symptoms of the one sign: It is "the last Swan-song of a dying swan." In Fatima Mary already predicted that at the end Her Immaculate Heart will triumph. According to many messages, this triumph of Her Heart (and the Heart of Jesus as these two Hearts are inseparable) will soon happen. Satan knows this and in his last convulsions he still tries to destroy everything in his power. With all his might he tries to gain as many souls as possible for his kingdom. He does this with the utmost exertion and many fall in his traps. The smoke has even penetrated into the Church as Pope Paul VI already observed. Clear signs of Satan's work are e.g. the rebellion of the faithful and priests against the Pope and the Bishops; the global indifference of the faithful regarding the teaching and morality of the Church, the justification of politicians (even by Christians and Church members) of abortions and euthanasia; the factual morality practiced regarding sexuality, the permissive attitude of social and church leaders regarding the whole moral life of the people; the sects and Satanic churches; the instigated national and racial feelings; the greed for materialistic prosperity and gratification; the confusion in the ideas. The two great instruments of Satan at the moment are the "New Age" movement and the ideology of a "New World Order." They are imitations of God's plans, because also God wants the unity which the New Age confesses and also He wants a New World Order, but they are deceptive and fatal. New Age looks beautiful and peaceful, but it eventually opens up possibilities of people to save themselves: New Age does not need a Saviour. And the New World Order is also based on personal opportunities of people without becoming dependent on God's grace and order. Both traps will finally result in a great frustration, into unrestrained hate of oneself and other people and will ultimately appear to be fatal traps of Satan. Regarding heavenly messages, Satan is also busy to mislead mankind. There are people who will reject all messages of "the last decades." The messages are put aside with declarations of "mass-suggestions," deception or "mass-hysteria." These people put their head into the sand and think that their sound intellect needs not to believe in such concoctions of disturbed people.

There are also people who have just as an erroneous interest in all the messages of the last times. This interest does not come from a sincere will for conversion but from a sickly curiosity and show off business... it shows the messages have missed their aim, because they were not given to satisfy our curiosity, but to call us to a true conversion to Jesus Christ. Satan, about whose existence many rational and modernistic people mockingly sneer, tries wholeheartedly to sprinkle sand into people's eyes and take care that the messages of Jesus and Mary are not heard and believed. This ruler of darkness is most content when people do not believe in his existence and thus do not believe his activities in this world, however much the signs of our time indicate the power of evil — "of the Evil One."

For believing people, people who take the Bible seriously as the Word of God, it should not be so difficult to recognize the messages as genuine. Indeed to everybody who is of good will Jesus promises the gift of the Holy Spirit, the gift of discernment, so that nobody can excuse himself by saying that he could not have seen it. Whoever asks receives and whoever prays receives the Holy Spirit. Or would Our Father in Heaven give us bricks for bread?

For whoever believes in the Bible as the authentic Word of God, uttered for the salvation and redemption of mankind, the messages can be very well-placed in the great framework, the great cosmic battle about which the Bible speaks from Genesis to the Book of Revelation. In the Book of Genesis the narration is about the temptation of Satan "to be as God" and "the Fall of Eve (and Adam) by being disobedient to the Word of God.

Ever since, man has become the battle scene of a heavenly battle between God and the devil. In this duel man is, however, very important. It is, however, not so, that this battle is made independent from man. On the contrary, it deals with the will of man who is free and can chose between the evil (THE EVIL) and the Good (THE GOOD). When "modern" man does not believe in the existence of Satan any longer, then herewith he has become automatically a victim of Satan because he has surrendered himself to his instigations and guidance. To illustrate the importance of our faith in the existence of the devil I summarize something that Jesus told Maria Valtorta in 1943, "It is pride and disbelief that make people nowadays deny the existence of the devil. Atheism not only denies God, but also the God-created Lucifer, the Rebel, God's opponent, the Tempter, the Jealous, the cunning, the indefatigable and God's hypocrite. The existence of Satan is not a fairy-tale of a silly old little woman, of medieval superstition. It is reality.

The so called "demythologizing" of the Bible has undermined the belief in the reality of heaven and hell. Also, this rationality has been a trick of Satan himself and man has been trapped into it as he could not stand the horrible reality. The word of the apostle: "Your adversary, the devil, is going round like a roaring lion seeking whom he can devour," is truth, is reality. And Satan transpierces our hearts just as Christ does. But he, the tempter, aims on our sensuality, our pride and greediness. He is hidden, cunning and his intelligence is much greater than that of man. The denial of his existence or the reckless confidence that man in himself is stronger than the evil makes man a prey and instrument of this "FATHER OF ALL LIES."

In this period, "the end of times," Satan tries to destroy our consciences as children of God. This rationalism has led to the level of human thinking becoming like mud. It is thinking in earthly levels, also about divine and sublime mysteries, which can only be understood with the light of the Holy Spirit. All that is holy and beautiful is being twisted round and tampered with through the false arguments of the human mind and finally it is still also justified. The historicity of Jesus' miracles is being denied, His Godhead and His birth from the Holy Spirit, the virginity of Mary, the true presence of Christ in the Eucharist, the Resurrection and Life everlasting, all and all is being demythologized and robbed of her reality. It is a very distinct sign of the "end of times."

God has created all things for man to be steward over. The whole of creation is for the sake of man. Man is the crown and hight point of God's creation. The condition for man to live in harmony or in order with creation, himself and with God was that he would obey the Word of God. Also, this was love of God. He did not want to put restrictions on man for the sake of power consideration. He put this restriction on man out of love, because He knew, that it would not profit for man to have knowledge of Good and Evil. Through disobedience, through the trick of the devil, the original harmony has been disturbed and mankind has been directed towards self-destruction.

In the course of history the pride has increased and has reached its fullness. Mankind stands on the point of self-destruction. The measure is full... At this point of history Heaven steps in and Jesus and Mary come with countless messages to announce a new period. Jesus' second coming on earth is near and the heavenly messages have no other purpose than to convince people of it and to help them to endure the great purification and to show them how to save themselves from this deteriorated generation. As the first coming of Jesus was prepared and made possible through Mary, thus it will also be at the second coming. Only through Mary can we escape the great trial and the purification which mankind is experiencing and is still awaiting. Urgent, urgent, urgent are the appeals of Mary and contain still the same: convert yourself to Christ, pray, pray, pray, renounce the world, fast, read the Holy Scripture, live the Sacraments with faith. Opponents of certain apparitions quote these consequent repetitions of the messages of Mary as a sign of "spuriousness." It is just the enormous love of Mary which wants again and again to indicate to mankind the essentials, wants again and again to appeal to "the only necessary," because the heart of man is so hardened, that it is necessary to stress the same thing again and again. And when we are honest, then we ourselves have to acknowledge that we often are lukewarm in prayer, that we very easily forget our good intentions to live our Christian life more seriously and intensely. We have always to be animated fresh again. Mary also reveals to us the things that await us. She predicts the coming trial and purification as never has been before and as never will happen again.

The first sign of this purification is the great confusion which exists. This confusion, as has been said before, has also spread itself in the Church, which consequently cannot radiate the Light of Truth any more, which is Christ. Everything that has to do with Dogma, the teaching of the Sacraments and discipline, has been made obscure by a very dangerous theory. The underlying fallacy, the ideology is that this would be the way to restrict the Truth of our modern world and to verbalize the modern thinking. It is a fallacy, because the Truth, Christ, and His Gospel is the same yesterday, today, and tomorrow. The Eucharist is Christ Himself. His glorified Body and Blood, which has been given us as food for life everlasting. Thus it was at the Last Supper, thus it was in the Middle Ages, thus it is in our century and thus it will be as long as the Church exists on earth. And thus it is with all truths of our Faith, which have been defined and fixed for all centuries throughout the Church. The purification will take place here and is taking place already to let radiate the clarity and simplicity of the Truth once again clearly.

The second sign of purification is lack of discipline. All Church regulations regarding Liturgy, regarding the duties of religious or priestly status, regarding the directions about social and moral life have been put aside. It is the lowest refusal to seek and fulfil the Will of God in life. Priests have also accommodated themselves mostly to the social values and norms. They neglect their prayer life and submerge themselves in empty activity. Rebellion against Canon Laws, celibacy and the rashly submitting themselves to one's own taste and pleasing themselves are the result.

The third sign of the purification is the division. We speak here only about God's Church; all the signs of the purification are also to be seen in the world, but they are most horrific in the Church, while the Church should radiate Christ Himself. The division in the Church is greater then ever before. And then it is in most cases not even about external division. Of course this is also there, but much more vicious is the division which lives in the hearts of many priests and even bishops and cardinals. Outwardly one confirms the unity with the Pope, the Vicar of Christ, but inwardly one opposes his declarations and directions. And outwardly — in life and preaching — one nurses an opposition against everything that comes from the Pope. In many aspects the Netherlands is leading. In the Netherlands there is a continual rebellion against the Church Hierarchy even organised, and many priests and other professional workers in the Church are participating in it. It is a continual undermining of the faith and discipline of the Church under the cover of an outward unity. One can never make these people more angry then by saying that they are not Catholic any more. The outward unity has to be preserved, because one is unconsciously aware, that the sting has been taken from their poison and they are doomed for ever. It is a great suffering of the Mystical Body of Christ, it is the laceration of Christ Himself, through which the faithful get into great confusion and turn their back upon the Church.

The fourth sign — also in relation to the Church — is the persecution which the Church undergoes. This persecution not only comes from outside — in many sneaky and masked ways — but also from inside. From outside the Church is persecuted by taking away Her freedom or preventing the proclaiming of Christ's teaching in public. In some countries it is forbidden and perilous to be a Christian. The persecutions are sometimes masked, sometimes also public and violent. But the Church is also persecuted from within. Within the Church there are among Her ministers those who have compromised themselves with the Adversary of the Church. Religious often experience opposition and ridicule from their fellow brethren only for the fact that they are loyal to the Church. Also in this, the Netherlands takes the lead. When the faithful would like to make use of the church eg to pray the Rosary, they then experience all kinds of objections. But when there is a request in favour of a "Rose Saturday" (in the battle for equal rights for the homosexuals on all fronts), the pastors open their churches eagerly and wide open.

All these signs indicate that the hour of purification has come. For the Church it is the same as it is for the world. Jesus and Mary have revealed this and they do this still every day. Ultimately, the merciful love of Jesus and the Immaculate Heart of Mary will triumph over everything. Ultimately, the messages are messages of salvation which deny nothing or excuse nothing of the coming horrors, but which indicate to man, who is open-hearted and who lets his pride be crushed, the joy of a new period.

In the heavenly plan, which is revealed by the many messages, Mary is the Leader of the army which will defeat Satan and his henchmen for good. All people who consecrate themselves to her Immaculate Heart and put themselves under Her protection, have the promise that nothing will happen to them. "Remain in peace, remain in the light, let yourself not be disturbed by anything, whatever happens," is often the contents of Mary's messages. Pray, fast, have confidence and live your faith and love.

It is for the simple faithful, for him or her who understands the greatness of Mary and the love of Jesus, not so difficult to understand the heavenly logic of this Jesus' triumph, prepared and cooperated by Mary. In Catholic tradition it has always been a certainty: that Mary has destroyed the "NO" of Eve; that the Immaculate Conception of Mary was the greatest miracle of God to make the Incarnation of His Son possible; and that this immaculate creature, this "nothing" would be stronger than the powers of the Evil. In the Apocalypse is the head of the snake being crushed by the Woman.

Already in Genesis God says to the snake (to Satan), that "He has made enmity between him and the woman." Regarding His creatures, God shows preference to the woman; Sin came into the world through a woman, the masterpiece of the creation through which God could become Man to nullify the Fall which happens also through woman: Mary. And as Mary preceded Christ in the historical period of their earthly life, thus She will also precede the second coming of Christ, which means the beginning of new period.

Already in Fatima, at the beginning of this century, Mary foretold the final triumph of the Immaculate Heart. In different apparitions She has hinted at this. The most important messages which Mary has given about this seem to us to be the messages of "the Lady of all Nations" in Amsterdam. Here lies the key of the triumph of the Immaculate Heart of Mary and the beginning of a new period. For several reasons it is like this: Firstly, there is the title under which Mary has made known Herself "The Lady of all Nations." All other titles which in the course of centuries Mary has received, indicate something specific. The titles refer to a certain group of people (Queen of Martyrs, Queen of the Apostles etc.) they refer to a certain quality of Mary (Mystical Rose, Tower of Ivory etc.) they refer to a certain need (Refuge of Sinners, Comforter of the Afflicted etc.) or still to something else specific (Queen of the Rosary, Tower of David etc.). Only the title "the Lady of all Nations" together with the title "Mother of God" are universal. The title "Lady of all Nations" expresses most deeply who Mary is, to which capacity God has raised Her and is seamlessly connected with the dogma which She predicts. For Christ has died for all people, He has come for the salvation of all and He has carried the sins of all people. When Mary will thus be acknowledged as Co-redemptrix, then She is naturally also "the Lady of all Nations."

The name "Lady" is in this respect also significant. Not "Queen" or "Mother" (though this addition is also found in the messages to describe the nature of the "The Lady") or any other title, but "Lady." The title "Lady" is quite universal. In every culture or nation there are women and thus the title "Lady of all Nations" is also linked up with the universally human desire to know "The Lady" in whom "being a woman" is revealed inviolate.

The addition "who once was Mary" (as it is given in the Lady's prayer) is connected and covers the dogma to a certain extent. It is not about a dogma of the historical Mary of Nazareth. It is about a dogma of Mary who was glorified and exalted by God, about Mary of the present. The addition "who once was Mary" shows this; without asserting, of course, with this, that "the Lady of all Nations" is someone else than Mary of Nazareth, the Mother of Jesus. It is as with Jesus Himself, who was exalted by God to the glorified Christ, the King of the universe, to whom all power has been given, without asserting that This One is someone else than the historical Jesus of Nazareth. It is like with us: We have the promise of a new life, of the resurrection "of our body" (that is of our person). We will be "new people" with a glorified body without asserting that we will be "other people" than our historical personality. We remain in all eternity the same person.

Further, the fact that Mary has chosen Amsterdam for Her most important messages is also not accidental and without significance. As Mary Herself says in the messages. She has chosen Amsterdam on account of the Miracle of Amsterdam in 1345. In that year a sick man received the Communion of the sick at home. After he had consumed the Sacred Host, he had to vomit and the matter vomited was thrown into the fire. Next day the Sacred Host floated undamaged in the flames. It was deposited in a box and the informed parish priest came to fetch It. The next day the Host was again in the box and this repeated once again the following day. Again and again the Host was brought back to the church and at the third time the parish priest understood, that Heaven wanted, that a church should be built in honour of the Blessed Sacrament.

That has happened and there came into existence, a yearly pilgrimage to Amsterdam in honor of the Blessed Sacrament. Until this day this pilgrimage still exists, a yearly "Silent Procession" during the night through the center of Amsterdam. On account of this Amsterdam got the name of "Miracle-town" and has always been connected with the Eucharist. It is also just the Eucharist, which is in many messages very explicitly mentioned, not only those of Amsterdam, but also at many other apparitions. The faith in the Eucharist as the Sacrament in which Christ really gives Himself to the faithful is of immense importance. It is one of the signs of the end and Mary calls the priests to return to "the daily miracle" She urges the faithful to go frequently to Holy Mass in great faith. Thus, there is a great logic that Mary has chosen Amsterdam on account of "Amsterdam — Miracle-town."

In the last century Saint Don Bosco received a vision about the Church of our century. He saw a big ship on which stood the Pope together with cardinals and bishops. The huge ship was attacked from all sides by many small ships. The big ship had two columns in front of her: Above the one floated a sacred Host with a shield on the column with the words "Salus Credentiun." (Salvation of the Faithful); On the other column stood a statue of Our Lady and there hung a shield with the words "Auxilium Christianorum" (Help of the Christians). When the ship was anchored to the columns and the columns came forward, the enemies got into a panic, and they started to fight each other, destroy each other or tried to find a safe departure. It is not so difficult to see this vision of Don Bosco in our days being fulfilled. It is exactly the Holy Eucharist and Mary who are the target of attacks. Whatever the Church teaches about the Eucharist and Mary and always has taught so, is being denied or re-interpreted. The simple belief in the Virginity of Mary has in our days become an enormous block of scandal... How is it possible that "learned theologians" cannot see this? Meanwhile, the denial of Her virginity makes the whole Incarnation ridiculous; it takes away all ground from the faith which ultimately is essential. God Himself has become Man in Jesus Christ. From the oldest creeds the Church has formulated that Jesus Christ is born from the Virgin Mary and the Church has always understood this literally. The permanent virginity of Mary has even been declared a Dogma and is also totally logical. Whoever denies this — with an appeal to the human aspect of Mary and to the "saintly" aspect of the human sexuality indicated by this, has understood nothing about Mary. Said between us, whoever denies the virginity of Mary, has also understood nothing about the true holiness of the human sexuality and about the true humility of Mary.

Also, the faith in the true presence of Christ in the Eucharist is — in other forms than in the past — subject to the most vicious and sneaky attacks. Among all the nice words is but one "belief" hidden: it is purely symbolic and by this all power and all meaning is taken away from the Eucharist. It is quite understandable that Mary has chosen Amsterdam for Her most important messages, in light of the title "Amsterdam, Miracle-town." But there are still other reasons why Mary has chosen Amsterdam as the place for Her purpose. Amsterdam, is as many European capitals, (but also in a special way) a melting-pot of all kinds of races and nations. Amsterdam is really a multi-cultural, multi-rational society. Amsterdam is always also a bit proud about the fact that the tolerance with the foreigners is great. One can hardly think of a better place than in Amsterdam where Mary "the Lady of all Nations" could be. Furthermore, Amsterdam is the place where the signs of the final period are most visible. The social tolerance here goes even so far that there is also talk about "Amsterdam, homo-city," where pornography and prostitution are for sale as a normal article.

Also the church in Amsterdam — except some "Rome-loyal" churches and some religious groups — is a very rebellious church. What is normal in Amsterdam in the church life is often in direct conflict with the directions of the Pope and the Bishops. Especially with regard to the Holy Eucharist, one can experience all kinds of things which shows complete inconceivableness of what in fact is really going on. I know from my own experience that everything that comes from the Pope and Bishops goes automatically into the wastepaper basket and that they want to be an autonomous church, that means independent from the Bishop. Also in this point, they will never admit this officially because they intuitively sense that they undermine their own right of existence. It is significant that the messages of "the Lady of all Nations" in Amsterdam itself, the place where they were given and where a chapel exists in her honor, are hardly known and hardly any attention given to them. If there is one place where a new birth of the Church is needed, then it is Amsterdam.

There is something else very remarkable in relation to Amsterdam and the messages of the Lady. In the book with the locutions of Mary to Don Gobbi, Mary declares a part of the Apocalypse, viz. Chapter 13 about the number of the Beast. Mary explains this chapter by clarifying, that the number 333 refers to God, to His mysteries, one times 333 expresses the mystery of the unity of God. Two times 333 expresses the two natures of Jesus Christ, the divine and the human. Three times 333 expresses the Most Holy Trinity. The one who wants to put himself above God — Lucifer — is indicated with the number 666. This is the number of the Antichrist. One times 666 indicates the year 666; in this historical period the Antichrist manifested himself through the phenomenon of Islam. Islam denies the mystery of the Divine Trinity and the Divinity of Jesus Christ. The number 666 doubled indicates and expresses the year 1332. From a historical point of view the Antichrist showed himself in this period through a radical attack on the faith in the Word of God. In this period are the roots of rational philosophy, the exaggerated value attached to the human mind. This philosophical error has lead to the Reformation and to the destructive rational science which has no need of (the hypothesis) God any more. The consequence has been a breaking up into many denominations and confessions and a gradually greater loss of the true faith in the Word of God. Three times the number 666 indicated, expresses the year 1998. In this year — according to the different messages of Mary — the Freemasonry, assisted by the Church's freemasonry will succeed in her great plan to erect an idol instead of Christ and His Church. The statue of the Antichrist will be built to be adored by all the inhabitants of the earth. The Church will suffer the most horrible attacks and trials. It will be the height of the Purification and Affliction. The door will then be opened for the apparition of the man or person himself of the Antichrist.

1. It is striking that the period of 666 (the first period of the Antichrist) coincides with the conversion of northern Europe by St. Willibrord and others. Against the rise of Islam, Heaven placed the conversion of Europe.

2. It is further striking that the periods 1332 (historically the second period of the Antichrist) coincides with many Eucharistic miracles in Europe. Sacraments' Day (1264) and the miracle of Amsterdam (1345) are two known memories of it.

3. The third period of the Antichrist (1998) coincides with the period in which Mary reveals Herself as Co-redemptrix,

Mediatrix and Advocate and asks the Church to include this officially in the treasure of Her faith by means of a last Marian Dogma. The Beast will thus be literally crushed by the Lady. The head of the snake will be smashed by Her foot.

Here you are: the importance of the Dogma. Hence, Mary will do nothing without Christ, without the Church. The title "Lady of all Nations" and the Dogma have to be acknowledged and proclaimed by the Church. The Dogma will cause a tremendous uproar and an enormous battle. For many it will be an unacceptable Dogma and right through all Christian denominations there will be a tremendous split. In the messages of the Lady such an enormous battle is predicted that it is difficult to guess the truth of this prediction. It means the greatest humiliation of Satan when Mary is officially acknowledged as Co-redemptrix. Yet, Heaven wants it: To give Mary Her place in God's plan of salvation, which is Her due; To show the victory of Her Immaculate Heart also being expressed in the Doctrine about Mary; To give the Church a light that would expel all darkness and evil; To be able to start a new epoch of the Church and the world. An epoch in which the Lady of all Nations, who once was Mary, can gather the nations of the earth into the one People of God; in which through Christ's second coming on earth His Kingdom can start; in which the Holy Spirit is again being poured out and the hearts of people being cured and warmed, so that a lasting peace can be a share for mankind.

CHAPTER 2

MARY CO-REDEMPTRIX

In the beginning was the word;
The word was with God
And the word was God.
Through Him all things came to be
Not one thing had its being but through him.
The word was made flesh,
He lived among us
And we saw his glory.
The glory that is his as the only Son of the Father
Full of grace and truth.

The word that was made flesh is Jesus. The word is the second person of the Holy Trinity, the eternal Word of God in whom He expresses Himself completely. He is the Word through which everything is created and without this Word nothing came into being of all that has come to be. This creating Word of the Father is made flesh, has become man in Jesus Christ. From all eternity this was the plan of the Father. It is the unfathomable, unlimited mystery of God.

A mystery which exceeds all intellect and which can only be accepted, believed and admired, in great humility. Jesus is the "First born." As the First He has proceeded out of the thought of the Father before there existed anything else in Heaven and the planetary universe. The First born is He, because He has been born from the generation of Adam as all human children have to be born according to the Will of the Father; through propagation free from sensuality and pain. According to the Divine and the human order Jesus is thus the "First born."

To make this birth from the human race possible, God needed a creature who was Immaculate, not affected by original sin, in order to respond completely to the Grace. This creature was Mary. Mary is — as the Church teaches — only a creature proceeded from the hands of the Most High. In comparison with the Eternal Majesty of God, she is thus of less significance than an atom or rather totally nothing. Only God is however THE ONE who is in the strict sense to achieve His will and to show His glory, God did not need the Blessed Virgin.

For His being — God — He is independent from everyone and self-sufficient. In a free decision God has made Himself, however, dependent on the most Holy Virgin in order to achieve His plan of Salvation and from this course He will not deviate in eternity, because regarding His eternal plans of creation, He is unchangeable in feelings and way of conduct. For our Redemption the second person of the Divine Trinity has become man but in and through Mary. In the inscrutable plan of salvation of God, He first has asked the free consent of Mary through the Archangel Gabriel before the Holy Ghost has formed Jesus in her womb.

From the beginning of the Incarnation God has made Himself dependent on the cooperation of a creature, the "Yes" of Mary. The "Let it be done according to Thy word" is therefore a real part; an indispensable part of the Redemption. From the beginning has Mary made herself completely one with the Word of God. The same Word by which everything in Heaven and on earth came into existence.

It was, thanks to the Immaculate Conception, that this was possible for Mary. Even humanly speaking, the totally absurd becoming pregnant without knowing a man, was for Mary no obstacle to the complete "Yes" to the word of God. In principle with the first "Yes," the "No" of Eve has already been crushed, though Mary will still have to accomplish her "Yes" in her concrete life till the end. Thus, from the beginning of the Incarnation we may already speak about Mary as Co-Redemptrix. Not only as cooperator (as it is expressed in the Second Vatican Council) but in the full sense of the word "Co-Redemptrix").

Without her consent the Incarnation of the Redeemer would, however, not have been possible at all. "Co-operators" in the Redemption "are all people who do the good."

To cooperate in the Redemption all Christians can and have to participate. All Christians have to supplement what is missing in the suffering of Christ, as St.Paul says. The Mystical Body of Christ continues the work of Redemption throughout the ages. All people of good will share in this work of Redemption. By grace, all people of good will are cooperators in the Redemption, but only Mary has this totally and completely. Only she deserves therefore the title of "Co-Redemptrix" and by this she distinguishes herself from all other creatures.

What Jesus has said to Maria Valtorta about the creation of Mary's soul is beautiful and touching. Already here it becomes clear how far the soul of Mary distinguishes itself from all other creatures. "All souls," says Jesus, "are created from the thought of the Father who sends them — His children — to the earth to bring life into the born bodies. The soul of the most pure, however, did not exclusively come into existence, from the thought of the Father alone. From the 'glowing whirlpool,' from which Our Holy Trinity exists, depart Our Three Loves and merge in the central point, there where our Godhead unites Itself and is ablaze. There is the whirlpool of the love, formed through the Three united loves. Humanly speaking from that heart came the soul of Mary. As a spark from Our will of love, she proceeded from Our united loves and desires as Daughter, as Mother and as Bride. Creating Her We disposed into Her everything of Our own perfection, because she was destined to become a brick in the building of the true Temple, the Ark of the New Covenant, the beginning of Redemption that — as whatever from God — carries in itself the symbolic sign of the Three: the sign of the Triune God."

And Jesus speaks further about the Co-Redemptionship of Mary: specific work of the Father is the first stage of the Redemption through the creation of the pure soul which is destined to descend and bring life to a body which would be God's tabernacle. The second stage was made when through the work of the Spirit, this totally guiltless, beautiful and pure virgin melted the glow of Her being in love with God down into God's own glow of love. Thus through the work of the Spirit she brought forth Christ among the people. The third stage began when Christ dying on the cross had fulfilled His task (mission) as Redeemer. Also, then Mary was united with God's work and through the work of the Son she became the Co-Redemptrix with Him and the victim. Closely united with God and his Holy will she is present at every moment and every step of the way of Redemption. Without Mary we would never had known a Redeemer. For this reason the feast of the Immaculate Conception is also the feast of her Thrice Holy origin, because the creation of Mary originated from the heart of the Three Loves of the Triune God. She teaches us to sing the Gloria to the Eternal God Who in His perfect love for us, has performed these two all lovable miracles: the Immaculate Conception of Mary and the Incarnation of God's Son.

We find a beautiful confirmation of this miracle of God's love in the visions of A.C. Emmerich. At the birth of Mary, this great visioner saw the child Mary being presented in Heaven before the face of the Most High Trinity and being greeted with indescribable joy by all the Heavenly hosts. At that moment, already Mary was introduced in a supernatural way into the eternal mysteries and all her later joys, sorrows and adventures were made known to her, yet she remained a child. We cannot understand this knowledge of Mary because this knowledge came forth from the tree of knowledge of good and evil. Mary knew this all, as a child knows the breast of its Mother and knows that it has to drink from this breast. Mary cried after this instruction by the Divine Grace in Heaven.

Also, in limbo, the abode of the patriarchs where they were waiting for the Resurrection, the birth of Mary was announced and there was an unspoken joy with all, especially with Adam and Eve. It was now that the promise of paradise was made true. With this announcement the state of grace of the patriarchs increased, their abode became brighter and larger and they received a more workable influence and power on earth. It was as if all their labour and penance, all their efforts, praying, desires and lamentations during their life only now bore fruit to the full.

A.C. Emmerich even narrates about a strong movement of joy at the birth of the Immaculate, in nature, with all animals and also in the hearts of all good people and she heard a melodious chant. With the sinners, however, there was fear and remorse. In the district of Nazareth, but also in many other places in the Holy Land, many possessed ones exploded at that moment in attacks of rage and frenzy. Under loud shrieks they were thrown to and fro and the Devils were roaring from their mouths: "We have to retreat, we have to get out of here."

In Jerusalem the old priest Simeon who lived near the temple, was awakened from his sleep by loud shrieks of the demented and possessed. In great numbers they were locked up in a building in one of the streets of the temple mountain and were under the supervision of Simeon and other supervisors. Simeon lived there in the neighborhood and came running at that time to the square in front of the institution of the possessed. He asked one of the prison guards for the cause of that loud noise by which he awoke. The possessed started even louder to rage, curse and cry, that he had to get out and felt himself chased out from there. Simeon opened the door and the possessed ran out and Satan shrieked out from him: "I have to get away from this man, we have to depart. A virgin has been born. Innumerous angels have descended on earth who attack and torment us; we have to leave the people and we will not possess them any more." Simeon began, thereafter, to pray very fervently. The possessed was horribly thrown to and fro on the square in front of the building and the Devils left him. The prophetess Hanna and Naomi, a sister of Lazarus' Mother, who lived in the temple and later became the tutoress of Mary, were also awakened and informed by visions about the birth of an elected child.

In hell there was an unparalleled rage at the birth of Mary, the Immaculate Conception. Satan knew that with this birth his game was finished and that he would lose from this innocent. Only senseless rage, explosions of the most fierce madness were the reactions of Satan and his henchmen. In Heaven, however, there was joy so great that it made every human description impossible. When we still have to speak in human words and comparisons, then it was God himself, the Most Holy Trinity who went into raptures about the beauty of this creature. In the infinity of this "innocent nothing" God could express His eternal word, to such an extent that this word could become flesh and appear on earth as the Redeemer of the people. The soul of the Co-Redemptrix was created and with this also the condition to realize God's plan of redemption of man.

The "yes" of Mary to the Angel Gabriel, made possible through the protection from original sin, was in principle truly the victory over the "no" of Eve, but in practice this "yes" had still to come to complete blossoming and to its full realization. During her life Mary has thus, also, become Co-Redemptrix as Jesus has become Redeemer. This "being" of Jesus and Mary has been realized during their earthly life through a continuing and perfect unity with the will of the Father. Both their redemption-work has thus served the salvation of the people and the honor and glory of God, the Lord and Creator of all that is.

This chapter is about the task of Mary as Co-Redemptrix. For this we quote mystics, visionaries and saints from Catholic tradition just to show the grandeur and beauty of the soul of Mary. Straight away from her creation Mary was meant as Co-Redemptrix. To describe the beauty and uniqueness of Mary's soul, human words cannot satisfy. Only in Heaven will we understand the full depth and the complete beauty. Jesus says to Maria Valtorta about this: "Whoever sees Mary, sees God already. She is the Immaculate mirror of the Godhead."

In order to chant the soul of Mary yet so worthily — with the only purpose to show the reader that she is indeed destined from the outset and worthy to receive the title of Co-Redemptrix, we drink from the deep springs which Catholic tradition offers to us: Bernardus, Grignion De Monfort, Augustinus, Maximillian Kolbe, John of the Cross and others. In this chapter, however, we especially draw our sources from the visions of Maria Valtorta because they most directly contain the words of Jesus and Mary themselves about the creation and significance of Mary. For everyone who is somehow acquainted with Catholic tradition, it is clear that these visions in no way oppose the great spiritual writers and mystics from Catholic tradition. On the contrary, they are the confirmation and supplement.

Jesus is the "first born" as well in the divine order (as he is the first thought of God) as in the human order (as he is the first-born from man according to God's intentions). Mary can now be called the second-born of the Father. With the creation of Mary, God had a true daughter according to His image. The image of God was printed in Mary so completely and exactly that it was only in the first-born of the Father more perfect. Mary could be called the "second-born of the Father" because due to her worthiness as bride,

Mother of God and queen of Heaven, she comes second after the Son of God and as second in His eternal thought, which from all eternity found pleasure in her. God has created Mary for Himself and for the Redemption of mankind.

From her conception Mary loved, as she was full of grace, she possessed the plenitude of it and thus she loved from the moment that she had a soul. Grace gives light and knowledge to the spirit, which is taken away by original sin and mortal sin. Mary, the Immaculate, was never away from God's thought, never from His nearness, His love, His light, His wisdom. Therefore, she could understand and love when she was still flesh which surrounded an Immaculate soul which continually loved.

It is impossible for man to chant the beauty of Mary's soul worthily. Our spirit is stained by original sin. All our thoughts, however sublime and true, are stained by decay and deterioration due to the poison of Satan. How could we describe and chant the purity and virginity of the Immaculate?

Even the greatest saints and mystics from history who have jubilated Mary with the most beautiful words, which the human mind can express, give only a dull reflection of the true reality of Mary. In what a shrill contrast stand these hymns of praise in front of these banal, trite and perverted ideas of many present day theologians and even priests who want to degrade Mary "to our level." They interpret her virginity according to their perverted rationalistic principles and call it a "myth." They want to pretend as if Mary has lived a "common" sexual life, as the descendants of Eve, with whom sexuality has been degraded to animality. They want to stain Mary with our stains. Jesus' rage over this corruption is without limit. "When man despises Mary, he will be crushed," Jesus says to Maria Valtorta, and despising is not only a public despising. Despising is also the denial of her Immaculate state of purity, of her virginity.

Despising is also to take away her unique place which she has among the creatures. Despising is also the jealousy about the fact that she alone is the blessed among the women and that she alone has been found worthy to become the Mother of God. Human being, realize about whom you speak, when you speak about Mary!

Only a boundless, a limitless trust and a total consecration to her, who is our Mother finds justification in the eyes of God.

Mary is the joy of God, the revenge of God against Satan. Against Satan, who through his temptation has brutalised the whole human generation, no single power is a match for him. No single weapon of man nor his intellect can win it against his cunning and craft. Only an innocent, an Immaculate who only through a kiss of the Most High upon her virginal soul, became pregnant with the eternal word of God and bore a Son, crushes the head of this snake.

In Mary, God has put the perfection of an elect creature, a perfection so complete, that it has destroyed in every memory of humanity, which is susceptible to the poison of Satan. Mary is the Virgin, she is the only one. She is the perfect one. She is the complete one. She was thus thought out, created like this and remained like this for all eternity. She is the Virgin. She is the abyss of inviolability, of purity, of grace which gets lost in the abyss from where she has proceeded; in God; inviolability, purity, most perfect grace. This is the revenge of the Triune God.

Against all desecrated creatures He puts up this star of perfection. Against the unhealthy curiosity this diffidence, to be only content in the love for God. Against the knowledge of the evil, only this exalted Innocence. In her is not only ignorance about the humiliated love, is not only ignorance about the love which God has given to married people. But still more. In her is the ignorance of the evil inclinations, inheritance of sin. In her is only the icy and glowing wisdom of the divine love. A fire which covers the flesh with ice, so that it would be a transparent mirror on the altar where God married a virgin without humiliating Himself. Because His perfection embraces her, who, as it befits a bride, is only on one single point lower than the bridegroom — subject to Him, as she is a woman, but without stain, as He is, still before sin existed God considered a means in His unlimited goodness to undo the guilt. That means was Jesus, the Word, and the instrument to make the means a workable instrument: Mary, and the Virgin was created in the sublime thought of God.

All things were created for Him, the beloved Son of the Father, the Word, which has become flesh to Redeem the flesh. To become flesh He needed a Mother. To be God. His Father had to be God.

And God created Himself the bride; the Immaculate woman, Mary. From her the universe may learn to love God. She cleansed the bitterness from the human disobedience, from the human fornication with Satan and from the human ingratitude. With her God takes revenge on Satan.

John of the Cross says about Mary: "The actions and prayers of the virgin, our beloved Mother, were always united with God. From the beginning already was she exalted to this high state. Never penetrated into her soul the impression of another creature; never was she urged towards something by such an impression. It was always the Holy Spirit who moved her."

John of the Cross indicates here that all the capacities of Mary, her feeling, her intellect and memory were completely "empty" from any impression which a creature had made upon her and completely filled by the love of God.

In Mary's life this is being expressed in very many ways. She had not a single "natural" desire, there was in her not a single desirability; not in earthly enjoyments, even if they were legitimate in themselves, but also not in a man. Mary was only directed towards God and her choice for virginity was as it were a self-evident, natural desire in her. She belonged only to God and it was a frightening experience for her when the priests of the temple decided that she had to marry. A.C. Emmerich saw that after this decision of the priests Mary confided her upset heart to God.

While she was in prayer she was parched with thirst and she went to fetch water from the pond in her little jar. Here she heard without seeing a visible apparition, a voice, as a revelation from above which strengthened and encouraged her to accept the state of marriage. Mary surrendered herself to the will of God and humbly accepted Joseph as her bridegroom because she knew that everything was possible with God who had accepted her now "to belong only to Him with soul and body."

But also in her marriage with Joseph, whom she loved very much in her soul, never has any impression of her husband been able to disturb the complete unity with God. However much she loved and appreciated Joseph, never has her marriage been a reason for the decrease of her total and complete consecration to God. This exclusive dedication to God has known a great trial, especially after the message of the Angel Gabriel. Moving are the pages, which Maria Valtorta dedicates to this. Mary already knew from the Angel Gabriel that she would be the Mother of the Messiah. She already knew about the overshadowing by the Holy Spirit. She had already felt the life of her child in her womb, but she was not allowed to say anything to Joseph. It was the great secret between God and her and God Himself would make it clear to Joseph. For Joseph, these were plainly intolerable days.

For us it is almost impossible to imagine what suffering, what confusion and doubts Joseph must have had, when he discovered that Mary was pregnant and also for Mary it was a suffering without limits, having to see Joseph suffering so much. The visions of Maria Valtorta illustrate this in an unsurpassed way:

Mary was startled by a firm knock on the door. She stopped her spinning wheel and stood up to open the door. How wide and loose her gown however was, she could not hide the circumference of her body. She stands in front of Joseph. Mary gets pale over her lips. Her face now resembles a sacred host, so bloodless it is. Mary gazed at him with a sorrowful and questioning glance. Joseph gazes with an almost imploring glance. They remain silent, gazing at each other.

Then Mary opens her mouth: "At this hour, Joseph? Do you need anything? What do you want to tell me? Come in." Joseph enters and closes the door. He still says nothing: "Speak Joseph! What do you want from me?" "Your pardon." Joseph bends down as if he wanted to kneel down but Mary, otherwise always reserved to touch him, firmly holds his shoulders and prevents him. The color in the face of Mary changes continuously. Now she is totally red, then again snow-white as before. "My pardon?" I have to forgive you nothing Joseph. I have to thank you still for everything you have done here during my absence and for the love which you give me." Joseph looks at her and I see two big tears growing in the sockets of his deep eyes. They stand there as if on the brim of a glass and then roll down over his cheeks and beard. "Forgive me, Mary, I have mistrusted you. Now I know. I am not worthy to possess such a great treasure. I have failed in the love, I have accused you in my heart, without right have I accused you, because I did not ask you for the truth. I have failed before the law of God, because I have not loved you as I love myself." "O no, you have not failed me!" "Yes, I did Mary! If I would have been accused of such an offense, I would have defended myself, but you... I have not permitted you to defend yourself, because I was at the point to take decisions without consulting you. I have failed you by permitting you to have the offense of suspicion. A suspicion is already an offense, Maria. Whoever suspects does not know and I did not know you as I should have. But due to sorrow I have had ... three days of torture, forgive me, Mary." "I have nothing to forgive you, but on the contrary, I ask your forgiveness for the pain which I have caused you." "O, yes, that was a torture! What a pain! Look; this morning somebody has said to me that I have become white on the temples and that I have wrinkles on my face. These days have been more than ten years of my life! But why, Mary, have you been so humble to be silent, over against me, your bridegroom, about your election and have you permitted that I suspected you?"

Joseph does not kneel anymore he stands there so bowed down as it were, that Mary laid her small hand on his head and smiles. It is as if she gives him forgiveness and she says; "If I had not been perfect, I would not have deserved to receive the Expected to redeem the guilt of pride, which has made man fall and then I have obeyed... God has required this obedience from me. It has cost me a lot ... because of you and because of the pain which you have suffered, But I could do nothing else but to obey. I am the handmaid of God and servants do not discuss about commands which they receive. They fulfill them, Joseph, even if they cost bleeding tears." Mary cries softly, while she says this; so softly that Joseph still bowing down, does not notice it till a tear falls on the ground. Now he lifts up his head and — it is the first time that I see him doing this — he closes the slender hands of Mary into his brown and strong hands and kissed the tops of the rose slender fingers, which appear like buds of peach blossoms from the clasp of Joseph's hands.

Mary is the handmaid of the Lord. Her whole life she had only one thought — to direct her heart towards God. Her heart was Immaculate, which means that her will was completely good and exclusively directed towards God. For this reason Mary has been obedient in everything, obedient to the will of God, whatever trouble she had to undergo. God inspired her to be a virgin and Mary obeyed. Whilst she loved this virginity, God asked her to become a bride and Mary obeyed. Also, this cost much because she was convinced that she would remain a virgin in the marriage life. She was convinced that she was destined for the loneliness within the state of marriage and the contempt of the people on account of her Holy sterility.

God then wanted that she would become Mother and Mary has obeyed, believing that it was possible that this Word came from God. Mary humbled herself totally. It brought the pain along because of Joseph's pain, her bridegroom. It brought along the pain of her Son's pains, which she foresaw and were predicted by Simeon. Mary accepted everything — the grief, the humiliation, the servitude. She kept nothing for herself and became the handmaid of the Lord. She became the handmaid of the Lord in the flesh, in her moral acts, in the spirit. Entrusting herself to God, not only in the virginal conception, but also in the defense of her honor, in the consoling of her bridegroom and in the seeking for a way to carry him pure to the purifying of marriage in such a way as to transform them, that they would give back the lost dignity to man and woman.

Mary embraced at first the will of the Lord for herself, for her bridegroom and for her child. She said "yes" for all three of them, in the conviction that God would not break His promise to help her in her grief as bride, in her being found guilty as Mother, in her giving birth to deliver her Son to the suffering. "Yes" has Mary said and nothing further and this "yes" has destroyed the "no" of

Eve to God's command. With this "yes" has the guilt been conquered. It is taken away and destroyed. It lies beneath her heel, it is washed in her tears, destroyed by her obedience. From her womb, the Word has become flesh. Flesh from her flesh. From her womb, the Savior is born. From her, the Co-Redemptrix.

Mary is the handmaid of the Lord and thus she is the "new man." The man is wanted by God. The total "yes" of Mary was still more than her body, the womb of the Word. Mary represented with her "yes" the whole humanity before God. She gave her consent for the redemption, by which she became the condition, as the consent of an earthly Mother and her womb becomes the condition to receive a child. The covenant which God once had made in Abraham and Moses with mankind is realized in the Incarnation of the Son. The "yes" word of Mary fulfils the last condition of the realization. The "yes" word of Mary is herewith a Co-Redeeming "fiat." It receives an infinite power and an infinite value by becoming part of God's redemptive plan. Because she uttered this "yes" to God, it is enlarged to the dimensions which correspond to the message of God. It is not only a personal "yes" — word, but it is universal. Mary speaks in the name of all who will participate in the redemption. This Co-Redeeming "yes" is also enlarged in time and becomes again and again actual in the actual redemption work of the Son. It is the condition of the Eucharist in which Christ again and again makes present His Redeeming suffering and dying. The limitless sharing of the Son in innumerable particles in the Eucharist is a mystery of substitution: His love is given way, His blood poured for the redemption of many.

By pronouncing her "yes" word Mary does the preparation work for the redemption of many. Because this "yes" word has been accepted into God's plan of the Redeeming grace, it has a Eucharistic character and Mary remains Co-Redemptrix as long as the Church — the presence and existing redemption activity of Christ in time — will exist. Mary's "yes" word and her function of Co-Redemptrix do not find their culminating point in the overshadowing by the Holy Spirit, but in the sharing in Jesus' passion during the Holy Week. It was already predicted by the old Simeon: "A sword will also pierce your soul." On Golgotha this word receives its full realization. To understand this infinite mystery a little bit, it is necessary to reflect a moment on the real redemption work of Christ. For this it is necessary to have some insight into the depth of man's "being lost."

In a time in which the stories of the Fall are stripped from all their power by labelling them as "mythological," it is difficult for modern man to sense the enormous reality of the Fall. Yet, it is a reality and indeed a reality of which the depth has to be understood in order to understand what Jesus came to make up for, why God had to become man. God created man as ruler of everything on earth except of God Himself and His angels. God created the woman so that she would be the companion of the man in the joy and dominion over all living creatures. God had created man as the crown of his creation. All the other creatures were only there for the sake of man. The stars and planets, which give light and seasons, each day, each month, each year again, as if they want to say "forget your limitation and look at the unlimited liberty of the sky: Let your souls come into ecstasy when beholding this great clarity."

God had made this liquefied blue for man. Just as the sea, the lakes, the rivers, the ponds, the brooklets and fountains which only serve to feed man, to quench his thirst and to cleanse him. The innumerable species of animals in all their splendor, the species of plants and flowers which look like butterflies in their beauty of color, the fruits and minerals. Everything is there only for one — "man." The whole of creation has added nothing to the infinity of God, to His almightiness, to His life, His happiness, His beauty. God had made everything for man to make him as king of creation. Man was allowed to live in this, in joy and gratitude, in freedom and happiness. This was the plan of God for man, with His creation.

The law of love, which God had laid in creation, was perfect, so perfect that we could not understand anymore the perfection of it. Man and woman had He created after His own image. Man was destined to live in carefree happiness, in reciprocal love, without fear, without jealousy, without concupiscence, without the threat of death. They were to enjoy their posterity; their children would be born without the difficulty and the pains of childbirth. Happiness and harmony were complete before the Fall.

The evil, however, that sprang up as a poisonous vapor from Lucifer's pride — God's most beautiful angel, came as a power, sprung from itself as some monstrous diseases spring up in the most healthy body. In the light-giving being of Lucifer this vapor of pride was nourished and condensed. God flung down this cursed incubator of evil, this stain of paradise, into the abyss. He remained however, the eternal incubator of the evil and while he cannot stain paradise anymore, he now does that work on earth.

The man had one restriction: He was forbidden to eat from the tree of good and evil. This symbolic plant presents the mystery of the people's formation. This knowledge God had kept for Himself. Satan has, however, seduced man to stain his intellectual wholeness with the knowledge of good and evil. He has (with his venomous tongue) fondled and caressed the limbs and eyes of Eve; he has aroused within them that which they did not possess before, because the evil had not yet poisoned them.

She "saw" and seeing she would taste. And Eve "understood," the corruption bit in her heart. She saw with new eyes and heard with new ears the habits and voices of the animals and with a mad eagerness she desired them. At first, she committed sin alone. Afterwards, she brought sin to her companion. For this reason the greatest condemnation rests on the woman. Through her, man became rebellious against God and has known sensuality and death. Through her, he lost control over the dominion of the spirit, the dominion of the morality and the dominion of the flesh.

The consequences of this horrible Fall of man were enormous. It was as if a crystal ball, beautiful in its splendor and harmony, fell to pieces and splintered into thousands of small pieces. The harmony in the cosmos and especially the harmony and the peace between man and God and between the people among themselves, was shattered. Through sin, death has come into the world, writes St. Paul. The consequences of sin carry cosmic dimensions: The complete order, which God had laid in His creation is disturbed through this. Man shames himself before God and others. He is from now on inclined to preserve his "I" and to affirm it instead of surrendering himself to God, his Creator, in strict confidence.

Man rebels against his own brother: murderers and thieves have we become, untrustworthy and untruthful. Sin has poisoned the heart of man and the human race has decayed through pride. Everything that God had created to enjoy in gratitude, has become filthy and destroyed. The animals have become enemies of man, the seas and lakes are poisoned, the woods and plants uprooted and killed. Man starts, instead of an admiring contemplation, to research the laws of the cosmos in a sickly curiosity and attacks with force the gates of Heaven and her mysteries. Pride grows rampantly and swells to dimensions by which man starts thinking that God is a recovered hypothesis or by manipulating and distorting God in such a way that there is only a caricature of His almightiness and majesty left. Mankind has been lost and has become self-destructive, but self-conceit forbids him to acknowledge this. The complete contempt of the truth, the good and the beautiful things drives man so far that in the insanity of his self-sufficiency and self-conceit, he prefers to let the world go to the dogs than to concern himself about justice, about love and faith.

There is, however, but one truth, which nobody can escape — man has to die. Only the agony of death and the fear of suffering still keep to a certain extent, the question and possibility of God open. It is truly the compassion of God that after the Fall, He denied man the entry to paradise — the earthly paradise. If man would succeed to banish suffering and death from existence, then life on earth would really become a hell without meaning and without prospect. The compassion of God has, however, spared us from this "because you have done this, you will have to die."

When we feel something of the drama of the Fall and the seriousness of the consequences, then we can also feel something of the work of redemption, which Christ has brought. Over against the disobedience of Adam and Eve, Jesus placed His unconditional obedience and unity with God. "Here I am, God, to do your will." The sin of disobedience could only be undone by God Himself, who became Man; because all people have the poison of sin in their blood. No man is able to live in total obedience and total unity with God. Sin has not only damaged the unity with God a bit, but also affected the deepest roots. Even the best among people are turbid and dirt in the eyes of God through the egoism which defiled their heart. God Himself had to become man to put an end to the dominion of sin, of Satan and to destroy the fatal consequences.

During His whole life Jesus has experienced the consequences of sin and it has been his daily cross: the hardness of the peoples' hearts, the unbelief and distrust, the bitterness and the lust for retribution, the ambition and stubbornness. Everyday He met these bad qualities of the people and also of His Apostles. Jesus' suffering was an on-going suffering during His whole life on earth. But on Golgotha it did reach its height. There came together all furies of Satan to destroy the Son of God in a last horrible attack. All hatred, all jealousy, all contempt, all pride and all self-conceit of all people from past, present and future fell as an avalanche upon the head and heart of Jesus. The Devil tempted Him extremely; the doubt about the sense of His Incarnation, about the sense of His mission gave cramps to the heart of Jesus.

He sweated blood in His agony of death, in a darkness and in a desertion of which we mortals cannot form an idea. The suffering of Jesus in Gethsemane and Golgotha is really the greatest suffering that has ever been in history. Here the wrath of God, the wrath aroused by the disobedience of man, came down in all its intensity upon the innocent, upon the lamb, that let Himself be slaughtered. The last consequence of sin, the desertion of God, was born by Jesus and it was a real God's desertion. God had really deserted Jesus on that cruel pinnacle of man's history, in which Jesus exclaimed: "God, my God, why have you deserted me." It is the unfathomable culminating point of His mission, the moment in which the redemption was realized and all guilt wiped out. Only Jesus, God and man was able to do so. And Mary.

Mary, the Immaculate, the Blessed among women, has lived this moment as all moments from the life of Jesus, in all its depth together with Jesus. Also, His God's desertion. The suffering of Mary was not less than that of Jesus. Two innocents who took upon themselves all guilt of the word. Here on Golgotha the words of Simeon, that a sword would pierce her heart became true in its ultimate consequence, in the desolation of Mary. Here "became" Mary Co-Redemptrix, the Mother of mankind. If the greatest condemnation weighed upon the woman due to sin, from now on it is a woman among all creatures who receives the greatest glory from God: Co-Redemptrix — she who has carried Christ in her womb, who has carried Him through her love, her prayer and faith, and who with Him wiped out the guilt of the people.

From her creation onward, Mary has been the Immaculate Conception, that means, that in her soul there was not a single trace of resistance against God's Word. Therefore, she is the "paradise" of God. God can only love Himself; also in the creatures He loves Himself, the image, which He has put on Himself in the creatures. Through the Word everything has been created and the Word was God. Thus, God can love only Himself. This is not an egoistic self-love, as we imagine ourselves with an intellect stained by original sin.

The love of God for us is true and real. God loves us, however, because He recognizes Himself, His Word, Christ, in us. This is not a decrease of God's love for us, but the contrary, God sees only the "best" in us. God loves us as we eventually, also, love ourselves alone. The rebelliousness in us over against the Word of God only calls for God's wrath and God's compassion. And also this is love: God is not angry because He would become less God Himself, but — because more than we ever can be aware ourselves — He sees how much man destroys his own destination and his own happiness.

In Mary there was no trace of rebelliousness. From the beginning onward She is totally ONE with the word of God: in her creation and in her earthly life. Mary is the prefect "yes" to God and the total acceptance of God's will for her. Theresa of Lisieux says that in Heaven God will do everything that she wants, because during her life she did everything God wanted. With Theresa this has happened in an imperfect way, because she is naturally stained with original sin. With Mary, however, this doing of God's will has happened in a perfect way. Mary has done everything that God wants and therefore God does everything that she wants in Heaven.

In a certain sense Mary has died, though her body has never seen decay of death and the grave. Jesus has experienced death through a terrible torture and He has really died. This was necessary so that through His death He would put an end to the dominion of death. Mary, however, has experienced dying as a sweet sleeping in the hope of the reunion with Her loved One in Heaven. The visions of A.C. Emmerich about this happening are brilliant:

> I saw the Apostles and disciples gathered around the couch of Mary. On Mary's face there was a delightful smile; it blushed as in her youth; from her eyes directed to Heaven beamed a Heavenly joy. Now I was a witness of a miraculous and impressive scene. The roof

above Mary's cubicle had disappeared. The lamp hung in the open air; my glance penetrated as it were through an opened Heaven into the Heavenly Jerusalem. Two luminous circles descended as brilliant clouds and in them I saw many faces of angels. Between these clear clouds, a beacon of light came down on Mary. I saw the mountain of light, which began with Mary, go upwards into the Heavenly Jerusalem.

She stretched out her arms with an infinite desire and I saw her body, totally wrapped in her clothing, floating so high above her couch that one could look through between them both and in that moment I saw her soul as a small, infinitely pure luminous form with outstretched arms, leave her body and along this route of light, that as a brilliant mountain ascended to Heaven, float upward. The two choirs of angels united themselves below her soul and separated her from her body. At the moment of separation they crossed the arms on her breast and her body again descended to the couch. My glance followed her soul along that way of light and I saw her floating into the Heavenly Jerusalem up to before the throne of the Most Holy Trinity. I saw innumerable souls, among whom I recognised many patriarchs and also Joachim, Anna, Joseph, Elizabeth, Zechariah and John the Baptist, who came to welcome Her with a reverential joy. She, however, floated between all these souls up to before the throne of God and her Son, who emitted beams of light from His wounds, the light that went out from His whole appearance. With divine love He welcomed His Mother and He held out something like a scepter to Her, while He looked down over the earth as if He shared the power and dominion of it with Her.

After the burial of the body of Mary, A.C. Emmerich narrates the following:

I saw during the night some Apostles and Holy women in the little garden praying and singing before the tombstone. A broad beacon of light came down from Heaven upon the rocks and I saw therein a glory floating down, existing in three light circles, full of angels and Heavenly spirits, who circled round the apparition of Our Lord and Mary's luminous soul. The apparition of Jesus Christ with radiating signs of His wounds floated before Her. Around Mary's soul I saw in the inner circle only small figures just like these of small children: In the second circle the figures had the size of children six years old and in the third of grown-up youngsters. Only the faces I could clearly distinguish; all the rest I saw only in brilliant figures of light. When this apparition, which I could distinguish more and more clearly, finally poured out itself on the tomb, I saw a beacon of light come into being which raised itself from the apparition up to the Heavenly Jerusalem. Now I saw the soul of the Holy Virgin, who followed the apparition of Jesus, passing Jesus' apparition, floating and penetrating the tombstone floating down into the grave. Soon afterwards, united with her glorified body much clearer and more brilliant, She arose from the grave and together with the Lord and the glorious multitude was floating again down to the Heavenly Jerusalem.

Thus, I did not see the Holy Virgin dying a common death and also not without dying ascending into Heaven, but before her death I first saw her soul being taken up and afterwards her body (united with the soul) taken up from the earth.

The "yes" of Mary receives definite fulfillment in the assumption into Heaven. Mary was dedicated to God with soul and body — which means with her whole person — and she is thus taken up into Heaven. Nothing of Mary's personality has been lost, her whole being has been taken up into Heaven. The old is not destroyed but transformed. Mary is and remains human in eternity but glorified. Through her sacrifice of her whole being to God and availability of her body at the message of the angel, Mary became a temple of God by the overshadowing of the Holy Spirit.

During her whole life, the spirit was active in her and at the end of her earthly life she was seized by the power of this Holy Spirit and as if in a divine hurricane sucked up to Heaven. Heaven is no place passing the borders of the universe, Heaven is a dimension of the reality — in fact the reality — which we with our earthly senses cannot observe.

The assumption of Mary is thus no separation, but on the contrary, she has deeper penetrated into the heart of our reality. As long as Mary lived on earth, she was tied up to space and time. She could not be present at different places simultaneously. After her assumption however, when her whole being, also her body, was glorified, were all limitations definitely broken through. She can from then on be simultaneously present at all places and this has cosmic dimensions. Her presence is a universal presence. Always and everywhere is Mary with us, she fulfills the universe; she is clothed with the sun, has the moon beneath her feet and on her head a crown with twelve stars. The assumption of Mary has not alienated her from us, but on the contrary, has brought her nearer to us. Mary is not assumed into Heaven to enjoy a quiet rest there. As long as there exists a battle between light and darkness, Mary is very actively engaged therein. Yes, she has the main role therein.

Jesus lives with the Father to plead for us and prepare a place for us, but He does this redemption work not without His "help," without Mary. Mary was the Co-Redemptrix through her life on earth, in which she had carried the Word of God, Jesus. She remains the Co-Redemptrix as long as there still is one soul on earth who needs redemption.

Our Lady of All Nations Who Once Was Mary

CHAPTER 3

MARY MEDIATRIX

I come to bring a special message. Deliver everything over well. Never has Miriam or Mary officially been called "Co-Redemptrix" in the community or in the Church. Never has she been officially called "Mediatrix." Never has she been officially called "Advocate." These three thoughts are closely connected. These three thoughts form one entity! Hence this will be the keystone in the Marian history; it will thus become the dogma of Co-Redemptrix, Mediatrix and Advocate and now I do not reproach the theologians when I say: Why can't you agree for once about this dogma? Once more I shall explain it and make it still clearer.

The Father sent the Lord Jesus Christ as the Redeemer for all Nations. The "Lord Jesus Christ" was this right from the beginning. He became this at the sacrifice and the return to His Father. Miriam or Mary became the handmaid of the Lord, selected by the Father and the Holy Spirit. Right from the beginning she was, through this election, the Co-Redemptrix, Mediatrix and Advocate of all Nations. At the departure of the God-man, Lord Jesus Christ, she first became the Co-Redemptrix, Mediatrix and Advocate. At the departure of the Lord Jesus Christ He gave in one gesture Miriam or Mary to all the Nations as "Lady of all Nations." Did He not say the words: "Woman, behold your Son; Son, behold your Mother."

One suggestion and Mary consequently received this new title. How does it only now come to the world as the "Lady of All Nations"? Because the Lord has waited for this time. The other dogmas had to precede, as life has first to precede the Lady of All Nations. All dogmas, which have preceded, comprise the life and departure of the "Lady" (from the message of the "Lady" of October 5, 1952).

The titles which Mary receives in the last Marian dogma — Co-Redemptrix, Mediatrix, Advocate — form one entirety. It is what the Lady herself explains in her messages and it is completely according to the Catholic theology and tradition. The "functions" of Mediatrix and Advocate are in fact a discharge of her function of Co-Redemptrix. When we especially speak in this chapter about Mary as Mediatrix, then this is nothing else than a further supplement and explanation of her being a Co-Redemptrix. It is as if one would say about a common woman: Mother, nurse and educator. The functions of nurse and educator are nothing else than a further supplement of her Motherhood.

> In those days Mary journeyed with speed to the mountain land, to a town in Judah. She entered the house of Zechariah and greeted Elizabeth. As soon as Elizabeth heard the greeting of Mary, the child leapt in her womb; Elizabeth was filled with the Holy Spirit and exclaimed with a loud voice: "You are the most blessed of all women and blessed is the fruit of your womb. Why should this great thing happen to me, that my Lord's Mother comes to visit me? For as soon as I heard your greeting, the baby within me jumped with gladness." Yes, blessed is she who believed that the promise made her by the Lord would be fulfilled.

The visit of Mary to her cousin Elizabeth is really a visit of Christ to John the Baptist. Both Mothers acted only as mediators. Elizabeth says that the child in her womb jumped "from joy." Through this move Elizabeth realized the presence of the Lord by the Holy Spirit and she credited this joy to Him.

Through the visit with the Angel Gabriel at the annunciation of Jesus' birth, Mary has become Mediatrix of grace. Through her the grace of her child streamed to the world. It is the power of the absolute obedience of Mary who does not reserve anything for herself, through which the power and wealth of grace of her Son can penetrate. Mary is always as she was at her visit to her cousin Elizabeth: The carrier of God's Son, she who brings the grace of the incarnation into the world, Mediatrix. Grignion De Monfort has also deeply understood this truth. He says that it is better for us that we approach God, not on our own steam and without a Mediator. This is, of course, witnessing a deep humility.

Our inner being is so much tainted through the original sin that all our qualifications would certainly be tainted if we would — in order to come to God and to please Him — rely on our own activity, capability and plans. These would impress God but very little in order to move Him to come to our support and answer us. Not without reason has he given us mediators before His throne. God saw how unworthy and incompetent we were and He had compassion. To give us access to His compassion, He gave us powerful intercessors before His Majesty. Therefore, it would be a proof of us having too little humility if one without recommendation — would directly approach God's throne and pass by these Mediators. One would then show very little respect for such an exalted and holy God. One would attach less value to the King of Kings than to an earthly king or prince: These last ones we would not dare to approach without the intercession of a friend.

On the basis of the redemption, the Lord is our Intercessor and Mediator with God the Father. Through Him we have to pray in union with the triumphant and fighting Church. Through Him we have access to the Divine Majesty. Without leaning on Him and without being clothed with his merits, we are never allowed to appear before the Father. We have to clothe ourselves as the young Jacob did, when he, covered with goat skins, approached his Father Isaac to receive his blessings.

But do we not have need of a go-between with the Mediator? Are we pure enough to unite ourselves with Him directly and on our own steam? He is God after all, equal with His Father in everything; hence, also, to the Most Holy we owe equal respect. Even if

He out of infinite love has wanted to guarantee for us before his Divine Father in order to calm down His wrath and to quit our guilt, then this is still no reason to treat His exalted Holiness with less respect and awe.

Let us, therefore, with the holy Bernard acknowledge without hesitating, that we still need a go-between with the Mediator Himself; and that nobody is so suitable for this service of love than the Most Holy Mary. Through her Jesus Christ has come to us; through her we have also to go to Him. If we do not dare to approach Jesus Christ directly, who is God, out of awe for His infinite greatness or out of shame for our nothingness and sins, let us then quietly call for the intercession of our Mother Mary. She is good and tender, not severe or refusing. Her exaltation is not that kind that she dazzles us with her splendor. In Mary we see our own mere human nature. She is not the sun, which hurts our weak eyes with her sharp radiation, but the beautiful and soft moon, which receives her light from the sun and tempers it thus, that it is not too strong for our limited capability. Mary is full of love: She will never refuse anyone who calls for her intercession, even if he is such a great sinner. The saints say, after all, that as long as the world exists, it was never heard that one, who with confidence and perseverance has taken his refuge to Mary, was rejected by her. She is so powerful that she has never received a refusal to her prayers: Mary only needs to appear before her Son with her request and He grants it promptly and He answers her prayer immediately.

Jesus cannot resist the pleading of his Holy Mother when He thinks about the breasts which have fed Him and the womb which has carried Him.

This whole trend of thought is borrowed from St.Bernard and St.Bonaventura. According to them, there are three steps to ascend to God. Mary is the first step: The nearest and easiest to attain. Jesus Christ is the second and God the Father the third step. To come to Jesus we have to go to Maria — she is our Mediatrix by means of her intercession. To come to God the Father, we have to go to Jesus. He is our Mediator by means of the Redemption.

It is a voice which arises from the history of saints and mystics who have understood and experienced who Mary is. A voice which is still to be heard in our times, but which is continually more loudly shouted down by the noises of those who try, under the mask of "modern thinking" to humiliate Mary and try to destroy her function in God's plans of salvation. The voice, however, cannot be brought to silence; again and again Mary triumphs over all the powers of darkness through her children until once, and the time is short, she will definitely crush the head of the snake under her heel. In our time, there are voices of the great servants and handmaids of God who give Mary the place of honor which is her due. Mary brings Jesus and Jesus is the life. That is her function: To bring Jesus and everyone who has understood this, understands also the beloved exclamation: "The Maria Numquam Satis," about Mary never enough.

Mary herself gives us the life, gives us God's Son and all graces with Him. We can never better project Mary's function, her mediatorship, than to let you hear a small fragment of the concert which is given throughout the ages in honor of her, our Heavenly Mother.

> **John Chrysostom:** "Truly a great miracle, very beloved brothers, was the Holy Mary always Virgin. Was there ever in the past or can there ever be in the future a greater or more illustrious one? Only she has surpassed Heaven and earth in greatness and what is more Holy than she? Not the prophets, not the Apostles, not the martyrs, not the patriarchs, not the angels, not the thrones, not the powers, not the seraphs, not the cherubins, nor does one find any other among the visible or invisible creatures which is greater or more splendid than she is. She is simultaneously handmaid of God and God's Mother, virgin and pro-Creator."

> **Anselm:** "O good Jesus, dedicated Son, you love your Mother and want that she is loved. Teach me, therefore, how to love her, so that I can be your brother, even if it were the last one.
>
> "O Mother who loves your child even to the beholding of His pierced side: You want that I love Him. Teach me then to love Him, so that I am your child even if I were the very last one."

Catherine of Siena: "O Mary, temple of the Trinity, O Mary, bearer of fire. Mary, giver of compassion. Mary, liberator of the human generation, through giving your flesh to the Word the world was liberated. Christ redeemed with His suffering and you with the pain of your body and your spirit."

Henry Suso: "Mary, you belong to God and God belongs to you and both of you play an eternal game of love which no power can ever break. Mother of the Heaven and of the earth, arise now and be Mediatrix and deliverer of graces before your tender Son, before the eternal wisdom."

Bernard: "God has willed that we would receive everything from the hands of Mary. Mary, Mother of grace and mercifulness."

And again **Bernard:** "Mother-virgin, daughter of your own Son, more humble and exalted than any creature. It is you who has made human nature so noble, that your own Creator did not despise your make-up."

Marthe Robin: "The Father has loved us so much, all of us, without exception, that He has given us His only born Son, and that He has given Him through Mary to give us a Mother Mediatrix near to Him."

Chiara Lubich: "About Mary one should not speak. One should be silent when it concerns her because such a theme exceeds our capacities. Mary is unique among all creatures, so exalted, that she is called the Mother of God and that she really is. Mary stands nearer to God than the people and yet she is a creature as we are. As such, she stands before the Creator and is for us as a bridge, which connects Heaven and earth."

Cardinal Pacelli: "It is but one word, but it has two sounds: Jesus and Mary, as the love of Mary is nothing else than the love of Jesus...; thus, the heart is purified in the school of Jesus at the feet of Mary."

Maximilian Kolbe: "Let us surrender ourselves to the guidance of Mary, let us be quiet, peaceful and not try to do more or to act more quickly than she wants. Let us be carried by her, she thinks of everything, she takes care of everything we need for soul and body. We should entrust to her every difficulty, every affliction also, as we can be assured that she takes better care of us than we ourselves can. Hence, peace, much peace due to an unlimited trust in her."

These are not all texts which directly speak about the mediatorship of Mary. But they are all texts which confirm the unique place and function of Mary in the plan of God's salvation. And this "Litany of Mary" could be extended, that it could fill a whole library. Never enough about Mary and it is really astonishing how little the present day theologians know the Catholic tradition about her or simply despise. How great is their guilt, because they do not acknowledge not only the function of Mary, but also they deny especially her immense grief through which she has become Co-Redemptrix, Mediatrix and Advocate.

During and after the horrible death of Jesus, Mary has suffered in a manner that nobody has suffered and that nobody will be able to understand fully. We can only imagine what the Mother of sorrow has endured in those hours. In His passion Jesus had only one single temptation, the temptation of despair. But the Mother, the Lady, did penance for the woman, who was many times guilty of every evil. And Satan raged against the victress with hundredfold cruelty. Mary had conquered him.

The most cruel temptations for Mary: Temptations against the flesh of the Mother. Temptations against the heart of the Mother. Temptations against the spirit of the Mother. The world believes that the Redemption finished with the last breathing of Jesus. But no! The Mother has completed her part by adding to it a threefold torture, in order to redeem. The threefold desire. Three days fighting against Satan, who wanted to bring her to deny the Word of Jesus and not to believe in His resurrection. Mary was the only one who remained believing. She is grand and holy also on account of this faith. Owing to her obedience till the end, her obedience to the Word of God, she has been exalted by God to be the Mother and Mediatrix of all graces. In an inscrutable way God has given Mary the power to mediate all graces which mankind needed. All graces, which have been given to mankind and to each individual being in the course of history and all graces which still are being given, come to us via Mary. Mary herself explains this to Don Gobbi:

I am the Mediatrix of grace. The grace is the life itself of God, that is given to you. It comes forth from the bosom of the Father and is merited for you by the Word, which has become man in my virginal womb to make you share that same divine life. For this has He presented Himself as ransom for you and, thus, He has become the only mediator between God and the whole of mankind. From the bosom of the Father grace has to go — to reach you — through the divine heart of the Son, who shares this with you in His spirit of love. As a beam of light, which penetrates through the window glass and accepts the form, color and the design of it, so also can the divine grace merited by Jesus only reach you through Him. Thus, grace forms in you His design, the same image and makes you more and more similar to Himself. The divine life can only reach you under the image of Jesus and the more He grows in you, the more He makes you resemble Him; in this way you can grow up as His small brothers; by means of the grace the Father shares Himself more with you, the Son makes you resemble Him, the Holy Spirit transforms you by realizing a life relationship with the most Holy Trinity, who remains increasing in power and activity. It is the most Holy Trinity Itself, who takes abode in the souls which are in the state of grace.

About this life of grace your Heavenly Mother is also concerned, because I am the true Mother of Jesus and also yours, I act as Mediatrix between you and my Son, Jesus. It is a natural consequence of my divine Motherhood. As Mother of Jesus I have been the means, that was selected by God, so that my Son would come to you. In my virginal womb the first act of my mediatorship has been completed. As Mother of yours I have been the means chosen by Jesus, so that you all could go to Him through me. I am the true Mediatrix of grace between you and my Son Jesus. It is my task to distribute to my little children the grace, which flows from the Father's bosom, and which has been earned by the Son and given to you by the Holy Spirit. My task is to distribute this grace to all my children according to their needs, which the Mother surely knows. I always practice this function. Yet, I can only practice this function completely for those children who entrust themselves to me in complete surrender. I am the way, which is necessary for everyone of you. If you do not want to go this way, then you run the danger that you go astray on your pilgrimage.

Nowadays many have wanted to put me aside, whilst they consider me almost like a hindrance to come to Jesus, because they have not understood my mission of Mediatrix between you and my Son. And thus it happens, that many of my children run the danger, now more than ever before of not being able to reach Him. The Jesus, whom they meet, is often only the result of their human researches and often correspond to their cravings and desires. It is a Jesus according to their standards: It is not Jesus, the Christ, the true Son of God and of your Immaculate Mother. Entrust yourself to me and you will remain faithful, as then I will be able to perform my task completely as Mediatrix of grace. I will bring you daily to the way of my Son, so that He can grow in you in His total plenitude. This is my great task, which I now still perform in silence and in the desert. Under my

> powerful actions as Mediatrix of grace you will con-
> tinually be transformed in Christ, to make you ready for
> the task which is awaiting you.

Mary has always been Mediatrix from the moment of her "yes" to the Angel Gabriel, till today. In the history of the Church and in fact in the history of mankind — she has mediated every grace which the people were in need of. In our period Mary is active in a special way to beg those graces for mankind which we, perhaps in this moment more than ever, are in need of.

For the last one and one half centuries, Mary has given many messages (almost always to illiterate people or children, so that the wise of this world become ashamed through the mouths of these "small ones"). In the last century, there have also been many Marian saints, of whom Father Maximilian Kolbe is perhaps the most well-known and greatest. Many congregations which have been founded in the previous century and in this century are dedicated to Mary. And special graces, which Mary has mediated for our time, are the lay movements. It is pre-eminently in these movements that the Marian profile of the Church has to be expressed. Mary herself was the laywoman and she is the model of the Church and namely that of the lay people. Among the many lay movements which came into existence, we mention two, namely: The Legion of Mary and the Focolare Movement.

These two movements explicitly have Mary as their "foundress" (the Focolare Movement is officially called "Work of Mary"). We take these two movements, by way of example, especially in view of what they say about Mary Mediatrix, the theme of this chapter. The spirituality of the Legion of Mary exists in two different points, which as a matter of course all have a relation to Mary. We read thus: "The Legion puts an unlimited trust in Mary, because they know that through God's decision she has an unlimited power. All that he could give to Mary, she has received in abundance. God has given us in her a special channel of grace. Through working in union with her, we will come nearer to Him. Thus we come to the fullness of grace, as she is the bride of the Holy Spirit, she is the way along which all graces come to us, which Jesus Christ has merited for us. We receive nothing except through her express mediation. She does more than only mediating, she obtains every-thing for us. The Legion is full of this belief in the mediatorship of Mary and makes it a theme of special veneration. For this reason it has taken in its Catena, which is daily being prayed by her members, the oration of the feast of Mary Mediatrix of all graces."

As further proof of this belief in the mediatorship of Mary, Bernard is quoted: "Let us look up a bit higher to become aware with what affection of devotion He wants to see Mary being venerated by us, Who deposited in her the total fullness of all good, so that we would know, that if there is still in us some hope, some grace or some salvation, we received this from her abundance which full of sweetness comes down over us."

The founder of the Legion of Mary is Frank Duff, a layman of our time. A man full of humor, wisdom and energy, but above all a man with an unlimited love and trust in Mary. He is one of the graces which Mary has given to our time.

The second movement which we mention is the Focolare Movement, officially called "Work of Mary." The spirituality of this movement has a totally different character than the more traditional lay movements. It is a spirituality which without doubt is of immense importance and truly still will be for the realization of God's plans with mankind, for the new epoch still to come. The spirituality of the Focolare Movement is not "devotional." Herewith is meant that it is directed at the first place on life itself and not on religious practices (which could be external). Of course, it stands in no single way in opposition to the other Marian lay movements, only the accent is different. The "calling" (vocation) of the Focolare Movement is to help realize the testament of Jesus "that all may be one." Through this the spirituality has a very ecumenical character, that means "ecumenical" in the sense that it has a relation to the whole of mankind. Though the Catholicity of the Focolare Movement stands beyond doubt — as the Church has also acknowledged it as a work of the Holy Spirit. This Catholicity is also in all her outward forms of appearance, less traditional Roman Catholic, but more universal (which in essence is the deepest meaning of "Catholic").

Typically Roman Catholic customs, such as the sacramental life and the praying of the Rosary — form an integral part of the spirituality, but they are practiced in such a way that nobody feels himself excluded by it, when he or she does not know or understands these practices. The Focolare Movement is, however, a spirituality of the "modern time" and as a charism it is one of the greatest gifts of Mary for our times. In the Focolare Movement the woman has also received statutory-wise the place which belongs to her. The president of the Focolare Movement will always be a woman to guarantee that the Marian aspect is also expressed in a concrete person. Chiara Lubich, the foundress of the Focolare Movement, could be called the "vicaress of Mary" as the Pope is the Vicar of Christ

The spirituality of the Focolare Movement consists of many points, among which Mary is, of course, one, yet the witnessing of Mary is different (not in contrast, but different) than in all other movements. To make this clear, we shall describe the "way of Mary," as the Focolare Movement sees this and where all members (but, in fact, all people) can recognise their own way of life and witness with faith. The way to Christian perfection, the way of holiness, for this the life of Mary is a model. All the stages in the life of Mary are comparable with phases from our own spiritual life. Chiara Lubich explains this herself:

> The first happening was the message of the angel to Mary and her consent. Mary was, of course, elected and prepared long before. But when the angel came and in spite of her fear, she said "yes" to God, something was born in her: The bodily life of Jesus took a beginning in her womb. In our own life there are people who come to us, as the angel did to Mary and offer us the possibility through their life, through an encouraging word or in another way to do something for God or to consecrate our whole life to Him. When we thus say "yes" to God, there is also born something new in our life. In a mystical way Christ is born in our heart and can develop and grow. The second happening was the visit of Mary to Elizabeth. Mary went to Elizabeth to help her, but at her arrival Elizabeth stood open for the mysteries of God. Mary immediately started to narrate and the result was the Magnificat which has resounded in all our Churches.

If we look at this hymn of praise well, then we see that Mary tells her experience with Christ therein, who already lives in her and gives sense to past, present and future. Christians have to realize that they have to start with loving in order to bring their choice for God into practice. As Mary went to Elizabeth, they have to help people who suffer and share their sorrow and joy. The person in need can then discover that in this Christian someone has come who has come for something more than only to help. There can then arise an openness to learn and discover the mystery thereof. Then the Christian can tell his experience of God. It can then become his or her own "Magnificat" of the great things which God has done to this Christian.

But there happened still something further at the meeting between Mary and Elizabeth: Christ's presence in the womb of Mary was so strong, that John the Baptist in the womb of Elizabeth was sanctified through it. This can in a modest way also become the experience of real Christians. Their experience can bring forth in the other person a change, a grace, a conversion, a meeting of the soul with Christ. Such an experience is something more than the history of an individual person, it is the blossoming of a flower on the tree which is the Church. The "revolution of Christ" can be experienced and understood in the small miracle of one person.

The third happening in the life of Mary is the birth of Jesus, which Mary offers to the world. This is, in fact, the heart of what the Church is. Christ has given the command to love one another. By bringing this into practice the promise of Christ fulfills itself: "Where two or more are gathered in My name, there I am in the midst of them." Christ is then spiritually present and this can be everywhere — in the factory, in school, in the family. These are then living cells of the mystical body, because Christ is present there. Where Christ reigns among two or three, man and woman, employee and employer, colleagues, or friends, there the Gospel can bring forth such a community life that the presence of Jesus can be presented to the world, as Mary has given Him bodily.

A further happening of great importance for Mary is the presentation of Jesus in the temple. It is a moment of joy, as Simeon says: "Now Lord, you have kept your promise and you may let your servant go in peace. With my own eyes I have seen your salvation." Simeon confirms that this child is the Son of God. But it is also a moment of suffering, as he turns to Mary and says: "And your own soul will be pierced by a sword." Mary will never forget these words and her whole life will be accompanied by a shadow of suffering which is not escapable. Something similar happens with every true Christian. First, there is the enthusiasm for the beauty and ideal of the Gospel. Then God lets you realize that there is an unavoidable condition to follow Jesus. That is the meeting with the crucified and abandoned Jesus. This requires a second "yes" to God, that "yes" to the cross. Mary, when she listened to Simeon, has said her "yes" for the second time.

The next happening is already an experience of the truth of Simeon's words: Mary had to flee to Egypt. There was a persecution, whereby the blood of many innocent children flowed. For the Christian this is a recognizable experience. The Christian life, if this is true, stands straight in opposition to the world, because Jesus is a sign of contradiction. There comes an inevitable criticism, often even by fellow Christians, who live their Christian life in a mediocre way. For the Christian it is then necessary to make his "flight to Egypt." To save Jesus, who lives and grows in the heart of the Christian, the Christian has to flee in the prayer and unity with the Church. The prayer is the powerful weapon against the attacks of the adversary and the unity with the Church protects the Christian from getting trapped in the many ideologies and opinions, which reach him daily from the world.

The following happening in the life of Mary is the losing and finding of Jesus when He was twelve years old. Mary then asked Jesus sorrowfully: "Child, why have you done this to us? Just think once with what pain your Father and I have searched for you?" This experience can be compared with the difficulties which Christians experience after the fire and enthusiasm at the beginning are cooled down. Old temptations against patience, against love or against purity come back again. These can be so strong that they darken the divine light. The Christian could also ask God in these moments: "Why have you done this to me" Why do you leave me in the darkness of your absence?"

The answer of Jesus will be similar to the answer of Mary. "Did you then not know, that I have to do what my Father wants?" These trials are there to purify you from all too human attachments. This experience of God withdrawing Himself is what is meant by the "night of the senses." Also, Mary has somehow experienced the pain of losing Jesus. When He was still a small boy, still dependent on her the whole day at home, she has lost Him. She did not see Him anymore, she could not hear His voice anymore and with her sensitive Mother's heart she could not feel His presence anymore. After this trial, Mary still lived a long time together with Jesus. Nobody will ever be able to fathom the depth and closeness of their common life. This also happens with true Christians. When the "night of the senses" is accepted and one is prepared to live in the darkness of His absence, then with the help of God's grace, it is possible to overcome this and to experience a new union with Jesus.

The following happening, which we know from the life of Mary, is in the beginning of Jesus' public life, at the marriage feast of Cana. Mary was ever present during the public life of Jesus, sometimes physically, but always in the spirit. Mary witnessed the miracles of Jesus and saw how He built up a community around Him. For a Christian Mary can also be a model. When a Christian lets himself be used as an instrument of Jesus, then he can see the miracles which Jesus performs through him

and the community which is built. The Christian becomes an onlooker of Jesus' work that he performs
through Him.

At the end of the public life of Jesus, Mary stood
beneath the cross. There the hour of the sacrifice has
come. She is not unprepared, there have been already
many indications. But a suffering that was foreseen is
therefore not less heavy. The most tragic moment is the
separation which is indicated in the words: "Woman,
behold your Son; Son, behold your Mother." Jesus seems
to take away from Mary, her own Motherhood, in order
to make her Mother of John, a person in which He saw
everyone of us. In an abyss of suffering Mary is asked
to give up her special claim as Mother and to waive the
fruit of her womb, which could be called her work, Jesus.
She has to give Him up as her Son and to accept Him as
her Lord. At that moment she is the deeply sorrowful,
the desolate Mother. The situation of Mary can make us
here think of what the mystics call the "Night of the
Spirit." Because nobody can better sense the agony than
she in the exclamation of her own Son: "God, my God,
why has Thou forsaken me?" Here Mary makes visible
the purpose for all people, whom God has had with her.
Her destination comes here to complete unfolding because at this point she becomes a partner of Christ. Her
suffering melts together with the suffering of Jesus for
the redemption of the human generation. The suffering
of Mary is the prize for her universal Motherhood. For
every Christian this holds true, that he gets his "Night
of the Spirit" when God has given him a special task.
Every work which God performs in a Christian has really to be the "work of God." Also, the "instrument"
which God has used for this work, has to let go of this
work of God and be detached from it. It is a suffering
that is very great and resembles the greatness and importance of the work which God performs in the Christian. In those moments can Mary alone, at the foot of
the cross, still give some light and strength. In her "yes"

till the end, the Christian can also find the strength for his own "yes" till the end.

After the death of Jesus the life of Mary goes on. She remains with the Apostles and fulfills her task in the Cenacle. She was the heart of the newly-born Church. In her was first realized what Paul said: "Not I live, but Christ lives in me." Mary became the Mother of the Church through her faith, through her expectation in Jesus' return, through her love. Also, for the Christian who has followed Jesus in this way, he too becomes Mother of the Church in a certain sense. Through his maturity, through Christ who is matured in him or her, he helps others to let Christ be born in them.

This spirituality of Chiara Lubich — a very Marian spirituality, is beautiful and of immense importance for the Church. For Mary is called the "model" of the Church, of the realized Christian. For the Christian it is necessary that he grows as much as possible towards the model. The way of Mary is the way pre-eminently to become like her. It is a spirituality "of the life," in which experience is totally central. In this sense, it is thus not "devotional." Also, the meaning of Mary's mediatorship is different. Though Chiara Lubich will never deny Mary's mediatorship in the sense that Mary is Mediatrix of all graces, "thus mediating graces from Heaven," the mediating which Chiara Lubich has discovered is much more a way of life. Mary "mediates" by showing the Church how she faithfully has to live. Mary "mediates" that concrete Christian being through her example. Mary "mediates" by being the first perfect follower of Jesus; the perfect one who till the end remained believing. The "mediating" lies here on another level, but is therefore not less "mediating." Certainly for the "new period" in which Mary shall take such a central place, it is of enormous importance to know the way of Mary well and to understand, as Church, how to follow this way. Chiara Lubich is then also a unique gift of Mary for our times and her influence for the future is not to be lightly over estimated.

At the conclusion of this chapter about Mary Mediatrix we dedicate a few words to one of the greatest graces which Mary has obtained from God for today's mankind: Pope John Paul II. In the book of Don Gobbi, Mary says about him:

> Pope John Paul II is the greatest gift which my Immaculate Heart has received from the heart of Jesus for your times of sorrowful purification. He is my Pope. He has been trained by me. Every moment he is being guided by me on the way of his personal consecration to your Heavenly Mother, a road along which he docilely goes with childlike surrender and great trust. He forms an important part of my plan. He is the pope of my light, that during these years has been able to spread itself in the Church and in all parts of this so threatened mankind. I myself guide him on all the ways of the world. He follows me with the docility of a child, with the courage of an Apostle, with the sacrificial spirit of a martyr, with the surrender of my Son. This pope is the masterpiece of my predilection and has the mandate to give to all the charisma of my Motherly tenderness.
>
> Now with anxious motherly fear I gaze on him, whilst my Immaculate Heart is touched with deep anxiety. How many dangers surround him. How great are the obstacles which my adversary puts in his way! Those who endanger his life are at the point to realize their dark plan. For him the hour of Calvary and of him being personally victimized comes nearer.

Mary loves Pope John Paul II very much because he has consecrated himself to her heart from the beginning of his priestly life, as she says. It is clear that Pope John Paul II is somebody who has consecrated his life to Mary. In every address or writing of his there is at least one reference to our Heavenly Mother and he is also the author of a splendid encyclical about the woman, in which is explained the significance of Mary for being a woman in a splendid way. This pope himself will have no difficulty with declaring the dogma: "Maria, Co-Redemptrix, Mediatrix, Advocate." From several writings of his it seems that he credits these titles without any doubt to Mary. As example, we quote here a part of a prayer written by Father Guerard des Lauriers which received an official Roman approval:

> Lord Jesus, Eternal Son of the Living God, we know that Thou accepted flesh in the virginal womb of Mary and that Thou has Redeemed us poor sinners by dying for us.
>
> From Thy Holy Heart, pierced by a lance of a soldier, St. John saw blood and water flowing. During twenty centuries streams of graces have flown from this inexhaustible fountain over sinful mankind, but Thou hast desired to involve Thy most Holy Mother, the Virgin Mary, closely in this work of salvation. Simeon had announced to her that a sword of sorrows would pierce her heart. From then onwards, she has accepted Thy sacrifice for our salvation; standing at the foot of the cross she became through her "fiat" our Co-Redemptrix and it is through her virginal hands that Thou extend to us all Thy graces.

In this prayer Mary has all the titles of Co-Redemptrix and Mediatrix. By the intercession of Mary, we may trust that this elected son of hers, Pope John Paul II, also will proclaim officially, that Mary so unbreakably united with Christ — during His earthly life and now in Heaven — that she is indeed Co-Redemptrix, Mediatrix and Advocate.

Our Lady of All Nations Who Once Was Mary

CHAPTER 4

MARY ADVOCATE

On the third day there was a wedding at Cana in Galilee. The Mother of Jesus was there and Jesus and His disciples had also been invited. When they ran out of wine, since the wine provided for the wedding was all finished, the Mother of Jesus said to Him, "They have no wine." Jesus said: "Woman, why turn to me? My hour has not come yet." His Mother said to the servants: "Do whatever He tells you."

We all know the result of this event: Jesus made a start with His signs and revealed His glory. He changed water into wine — the best wine — and with this He did his first "public miracle." It is striking that the evangelist John in the introduction of the story calls Mary twice: "The Mother of Jesus," as if he wants to draw the attention to this quality of Mary. The words of Jesus sound more striking: "Woman, why turn to me? My hour has not come yet." Or in other (better) translations: "Woman, what is there between you and me?" The addressing title "Woman" stands in a certain contrast with John naming her: "The Mother of Jesus." It is just by using the name "Woman" that Jesus lets us see that there has arisen another relationship between Him and Mary. The words "not yet" in the sentence is perhaps clarified a bit further: "What is there between you and me?" Till that moment Mary has been the Mother of Jesus. Jesus belonged to her in the hidden life of Nazareth. He had been obedient to her. He had been subject to her. From now onwards, however, Jesus belongs to His mission. And a new relationship has arisen between Him and His Mother. Jesus starts His public life. He is the expected Messiah and from now onwards, He belongs to His Father. Only after the completion of His mission and that of Mary's mission does Jesus again belong to Mary.

Jesus has purposely started with His signs in the presence of and with the intercession of His Mother. He also purposely calls her "Woman." Already at this first sign at the beginning of His public life, it clarifies Mary's part: ...She is the "Woman," the "New Eve" who cooperates with the "Man," the "New Adam." The part of the woman is to be Advocate for the people. In her motherly care and mercy she sees the needs of the people and she brings them to Jesus. She arouses, also, the faith and trust of the people in Jesus: "Just do what He will tell you." Not for a moment did Mary doubt the love of Jesus and the relieving of the people's needs. By way of speech, it has only to be brought to His attention. Mary lets Jesus be completely free in the way in which He will solve the problem. She brings the need to His attention and nothing more. She believes and trusts.

The story tells us something more about the meaning of Mary in the mission of Jesus. Mary stands here not only next to Jesus as His physical Mother. She personifies much more. The miracle at Cana can be seen as an example of the Eucharist in which bread and wine are changed by Christ into His body and blood. It is an example of the Church where Jesus distributes His graces freely and supremely. Mary stands here also as Mother of the Church next to the Lord of the Church.

Mary certainly is in the first place a woman who has the super-vision over the household in a female manner, observes the needs and has an eye for the smooth running of the feast. This she does from her natural, human womanliness and this quality Mary will always have. She will always see in the home of Christendom where the needs are and her part will remain to show her divine Son what her motherly glance discovers. Mary knows His divine possibilities and that for Him nothing is impossible. Mary has an unlimited trust in Him. Therefore, she puts no demands but only entrusts the need to Jesus: He will know how He can best alleviate this need. Here at the marriage feast of Cana, it becomes immediately clear the part which Mary fulfills from then onwards till this day — advocate for mankind in need.

The first miracle of Jesus took place through Mary. It symbolizes that Mary is the key to the miracle. Jesus refuses His Mother nothing and for the sake of her prayer He hastens the time of grace. He knows that after God she is the second in goodness and that she never wants anything else than what God wants. At the marriage feast of Cana, Jesus showed us Mary's power together with His own power. Mary was destined to be united with Jesus in the flesh, as they were one flesh: Jesus in her and she around Him. Mary was destined to be united with Jesus in the suffering as they were together on the cross. Jesus with the flesh, Mary with her spirit. Therefore, it was also Mary that was united with Jesus in the power which showed itself to the world. Mary has really received the power from God to be the Advocate: Nothing will be refused her.

It has always been the conviction of the Church that Mary is our special Advocate. The Litany of Mary has many titles which refer to this quality (or function). One of the most beautiful titles is "Refuge of Sinners." Just because Mary is Mother, as she is nearer to the feelings of the people than God, she is the refuge for all who are in need and especially in moral need. A big sinner hardly dares to trust the mercy of God, when he realizes his sinfulness (however much this is a misconception, one can understand it). But the people always dare to go to Mary to ask for her intercession. It is moving what Maria Valtorta in this connection saw about Peter after the crucifixion of Jesus. Peter is despairing due to his denial of Jesus and he thinks that for him no more salvation is possible. John has already tried to calm him down though he did not succeed: Peter seemed to wander in his despair. In the end, John managed to convince Peter to go to Mary. When Peter reaches the house where Mary lives, he does not dare to enter it.

> And Mary calls him kindly: "Simeon of Jonah, come." Nothing. "Simeon Peter, come." Nothing. "Peter of Jesus and Mary, come." A sharp burst of weeping. But he does not go in. Mary stands up. She leaves the mantle on the table and goes to the door.
> Peter is crouched outside. Like a dog with no master. He cries so loud and all curled up, that he cannot hear the noise of the door that opens squeaking or the

shuffling of Mary's sandals. He realizes that she is there when she bends so low as to take his hand, pressed against his eyes, and she compels him to stand up. She goes back into the room dragging him like a little boy. She closes the door and locks it and bent with sorrow, as he is with shame, she goes back to her seat.

Peter kneels at her feet and weeps without restraint. Mary caresses his grey hair, wet with perspiration of sorrow. Nothing but such caresses, until he calms down.

Then, when at last Peter says: "You cannot forgive me. So do not careesses me. Because I have denied Him." Mary says: "Peter, you have denied Him. That is true. You had the courage of denying Him in public. The cowardly courage of doing that. The others ... everybody, except the shepherds, Manaen, Nicodemus and Joseph and John, have been cowards. They have all denied Him: the men and women of Israel, except a few women... I will not mention the nephews and Alphaeus of Sarah. They were relatives and friends. But the others! ...And they did not have the satanic courage of lying to save themselves, or the spiritual courage of repenting and weeping, nor the more elevated courage of acknowledging their error in public. You are a poor man. Or rather, you were. As long as you relied on yourself. Now you are a man. Tomorrow you will be a saint. But even if you were not what you are, I would have forgiven you all the same. I would have forgiven also Judas, to save his soul. Because the value of a soul, also of one only, deserves every effort to overcome disgust and resentment, to the extent of being crushed thereby. Bear that in mind, Peter. I will repeat it to you: "The value of a soul is such that, at the cost of dying through the effort and suffering to have it close to us, one must hold it so, in one's arms, as I am holding your grey-haired head, if one realizes that, by holding it so, it can be saved." So ... like a mother who, after the father's punishment, presses the head of her guilty son to her heart and more with the words of her distressed heart that beats with love and sorrow, than with the father's blows, reforms and achieves.

Peter of my Son. Poor Peter who has been, like everybody, in the hands of Satan in this hour of darkness, and you were not aware of it, and you think that you have done everything by yourself, come, do come here, on the heart of the Mother of my Son's children. Here Satan can no longer harm you. Here storms abate, and while waiting for the sun, my Jesus, who rises to say to you: "Peace to you, my Peter," the morning star rises, pure and beautiful, and makes everything it kisses pure and beautiful, as happens on the clear water of our sea in the fresh spring mornings.

That is why I have wished so much to have you. At the foot of the cross, I was tortured because of Him and of you and — how come you did not perceive it? — and I called your spirits so loud that I think they really came to me. And closed in my heart, or rather, laid on my heart, like the loaves of the offering, I held them under the bath of His blood and His tears. I was able to do so, because, in John, He made me the Mother of all His progeny... How much I longed for you! That morning, in that afternoon, at night and the following day... Why, poor Peter, wounded and trampled on by the demon, did you keep a mother waiting so long? Do you not know that it is the task of mothers to tidy up, cure, forgive and lead their children? I will lead you to Him.

Would you like to see Him? Would you like to see His smile, to be convinced that He still loves you? Would you? Oh! then move away from my poor lap of a woman and lay your forehead on His crowned forehead, your lips on His wounded lips and kiss your Lord."

"He is dead... I shall never be able to do it again."

"Peter. Reply to me. Which do you think is the last miracle of your Lord?"

"The Eucharist. No. That of the soldier cured there ... there ... Oh, I do not remember it anymore!"

A faithful, loving strong woman met Him on Calvary and wiped His face. And He, to tell us how much love can do, impressed the image of His face on the linen cloth. Here it is, Peter. A woman achieved that in an hour of hellish darkness and of divine wrath. Simply because she loved. Bear that in mind, Peter, for the hours in which the demon will seem to you to be stronger than God. God was the prisoner of men, He was already overwhelmed, condemned, scourged, He was already dying ... and yet, as God is always God even among the most cruel persecutions, and if the idea is struck, God who inspires it is untouchable, so God to deniers, to unbelievers, to the men of foolish "whys," of the guilty "it cannot be," of the sacrilegious "what I do not understand is not true," replies, without any words, with this cloth. Look at it. One day, you told me, you said to Andrew: "The Messiah showed Himself to you? It cannot be true," and then your human reason had to bend before the power of the spirit that saw the Messiah where reason did not see Him. On another occasion, on the stormy sea, you asked: "Shall I come, Master?" and then, when you were half way, on the agitated water, you became doubtful saying: "Water cannot hold me" and with your doubt as ballast, you were almost drowned. Only when the spirit that believed prevailed against human reason, you were able to find the help of God... On another occasion you said: "If Lazarus has been dead four days, why have we come? To die in vain?" Because with your human reason you could not suppose another solution. And your reason was disproved by the spirit, that by pointing out to you, through the man raised from the dead, the glory of Him who had raised him, showed you that you had not gone there in vain.

Another time, many other times, upon hearing your Lord speak of death, and a cruel death, you said: "That will never happen to you!" And you can see how your reason has been given the lie! Now wait to hear the word of your spirit in this last case.

"Forgive me..." Another word. "ANOTHER ONE."

"I don't know."

"I LOVE, Peter, LOVE. You will be forgiven. You will believe. You will be strong. You will be the priest, not the Pharisee who oppresses and has nothing but formalism and lack of active faith. Look at Him. Dare to look at Him. Everybody has looked at Him and venerated Him... Even Longinus... And would you not be able? And yet you were able to deny HIM! If you do not recognise Him NOW, through the fire of My motherly loving sorrow that joins you and reconciles you, you will never be able again. He rises from the dead. How will you be able to look at Him in His new splendor, if you do not know His face in the passage from the Master you know to the triumpher whom you not know? Because sorrow, all the sorrow of ages and of the world, has worked on Him with chisel and mallet in the hours from Thursday evening to the ninth hour on Friday. And they have changed His face. Previously He was only the master and friend. Now He is the judge and king. He has ascended on His throne to judge. And He put on His crown. He will remain so. The only difference is that after His glorious resurrection, He will no longer be the man judge and king, but the God judge and king. Look at Him. Look at Him while humanity and sorrow veil Him, in order to be able to look at Him when He triumphs in His divinity."

Peter at last raises his head from Mary's lap and looks at her, with his eyes red with weeping, in the face of an old child, who is desolate and surprised at the evil he has done and at all the good he finds.

Mary compels him to look at the Lord. Then while Peter, as if he were before a living face, says moaning: "Forgive me, forgive me! I do not know how it happened. What happened. I was not myself. It was something that made me be not myself. BUT I love you Jesus. I love you master! Come back! Come back! Do not go away like that, without telling me that you have understood me!"

Mary repeats the gesture already made in the sepulchral room. Standing, her arms outstretched, she looks like the priestess at the moment of the offerings. And as she offered the Immaculate host, here she offers the repentant sinner. She is indeed the Mother of saints and sinners! Then she makes Peter stand up and continues to console him. And she says to him: "I am now happier. I know that you are now here. Go now where the women and John are. You all need rest and food. Go. And be good..." as if he were a boy.

The beautiful and living description which Maria Valtorta gives us about Mary stresses especially her quality as "Mother." Because Mary is our Mother, she is our Advocate. This is being confirmed by the experiences and visions of numerous saints from the history of the Church. In the notes of Adrienne Von Speyr one can, eg. read that the saints in Heaven also have their discussions. Whilst some, eg. Ignatius of Loyola like to recommend powerful means to put lukewarm and inert Christians into motion, Mary always appears as "Advocata Nostra" (our Advocate). She is always Mother and defends and tries to calm down the naturally more temperamental and energetic saints.

Of all saints Mary mostly shows God's mercy and, therefore, she is pre-eminently our Mother and Advocate. Many have experienced this. Elizabeth of the Trinity writes: "There is a motherly heart, in which you can hide yourself: that of Mary." Theresa of Lisieux narrates about her experience during her painful sickness: "I was completely hidden under the veil of the Holy Virgin. I have asked her to take my head into her hands." And, furthermore, Theresa says to her superior: "I would love to have a nice death, just to please you. I asked Our Lady for it. I have not asked God for it, as I want Him to do what He wants. To ask something from the Holy Virgin is not the same. She knows what to do with my tiny desires, whether she has to propose them to God or not... She has to judge the matter, so that she does not force God to grant me, but let Him do His will in all things."

If we have prayed to the Holy Virgin and she has not answered the prayer, then this is a sign. Then one should leave her in peace and have no worries. Grignion De Monfort expresses himself in the same spirit: "The greatest benefit Mary shows her true venerators is her intercession before her son. With her prayers Mary calms down his anger, units them intimately with him and keeps them in that union. Rebecca brought Jacob, to the bed of his father. The grey-haired man touched him, kissed him even with joy, because the meat, well-cooked and offered by Jacob had tasted very well. When he then had smelled the nice fragrance of his clothes with much satisfaction, he exclaimed: 'Look, the fragrance of my son is as the fragrance of a field, blessed by the Lord.' The full field, of which the fragrance brings the fatherly heart into ecstasy is the fragrance of Mary's virtues and merits. Because she is a field full of grace, God the Father has sown his only son therein, the wheat grain of the elected. Oh, how welcome is a child of Mary with Jesus Christ, the Father of the coming ages, when surrounded with her good fragrance! How quickly and intimately they become one together! Moreover, when Mary has once overloaded her children and faithful servants with her favors and won for them the blessing of God the Father and has them united with Jesus Christ, she keeps them further in Jesus Christ and Jesus Christ in them. With great vigilance she cares for them. Afraid as she is, that they would lose God's grace and would get entangled in the snares of their enemies. She keeps the saints in their plenitude and helps them to persevere therein till the end."

To Don Gobbi, Mary herself confirms her part of Advocate. "I am your heavenly Mother. I am the Mother of the intercession and the reparation. It is my motherly task to intercede every day for you with my son, Jesus. As an attentive and caring mother, I ask for all the graces you need to walk the way of good, of love and of holiness. For my sinful children I get the grace of repentance, of the renewal of heart and the return to the Lord. To my sick children I grant the gift to understand the meaning of suffering, to accept it willingly, to bear it with love and to carry their cross with confidence and in childlike obedience to the will of the Lord. For my good children, I grant the gift of perseverance in the good. For my son's priests, I intercede at best, so that they are Holy ministers who are faithful to Jesus and His Gospel.

Every new day which begins, corresponds to a new attitude of prayer of your heavenly Mother to help you in the desert of your time to go the way of love and of faithful fulfilling of the will of God, which has to be performed with childlike submissiveness." The choir of voices, who honor Mary as Advocate, and more than just to honor, they give Mary her due place, which she has in God's salvation plan, is not silenced and continues till to our day. Chiara Lubich says about Mary's task as Advocate: "It was Mary who at the marriage feast of Cana encouraged Jesus to start His public life as God Himself had also made use of Mary when the word became flesh. If we do not give Mary the place which God has given her, then we really are not true Christians.

The surrender to Mary should pervade our hearts. It should be normal for us that we go to her at any time, as a child goes to his mother. In our life we experience much suffering and grief and this all the more when God has entrusted to us a great task. That could often mean that we as Mary stand "at the feet of the cruci-fied" and not being able to deliver Him from His suffering, we have to stay with Him, without being able to do anything and in spite of this, we ourselves tremble with fear. It is the powerless "stabat" of Mary under the cross. To her we could say: "Mary, you know these pains, alleviate those who suffer. Use this hour of heal-ing for these people that you also love."

A great troubador of Mary in our times is Igino Giordani, a prophetical figure, ecumenist of the first hour and very knowledge-able of the Church Fathers. In his last book, titled *Mary*, he cel-ebrated in a moving way the beauty of Mary. The book is like a poem, but it excels also in theological solidity and knowledge of the great tradition, while simple people's faith is also interwoven. Igino Giordani lets us see that Mary is the strong and the limitless affectionate woman, just through her humility, a virtue which has completely nothing to do with powerless passivity — which makes her so powerful in her intercession with God. Just let us listen to this lover of Mary: "Humility does not mean softening as it seeks to the theoreticals of the dehumanization of Europeans who con-fuse power with boasting. Humility is the action with which one frees oneself from a heap of images which cover one's own misery, clothes one's own weakness with the bravery of gladiators and idle talk, if imagination and insanity are also not added to it. It is a deed of a brave tidiness to discover one's own weakness and thus to implore that this is strengthened with divine power, by impressing into one's head the will of God. Thus, one's own death is replaced with God's life: the first condition to move oneself in the eternal is to deify oneself. Our nothingness takes then part in the plenitude of God. If there is one woman in the Old Testament who resembles Mary, then this is Judith, a chaste widow of rare beauty, who has become the glory of Israel by liberating it from the tyranny."

The humility of Mary was the condition to be able to predict the crushing of the proud and the exalting of the poor with more power than the powerful: the revolution. But it concerns a power which, if God wants it, influences God Himself by the power of love. Theology speaks about the almightiness of prayer. Prayer now gets the superhuman value, when it sprouts from a heart which is full of the Holy Spirit, a heart that only beats from love for God. Here lies the power of Mary as Advocate! The Christian mysticism has always found it logical that "the heavenly King became the prisoner of the Immaculate purity, of her loving meekness, her tender beauty." "How could or would the heavenly King refuse something?" asks Heinrich Suso. The powerfulness of Mary proceeds from her unlimited humility, which is not a seat of weakness. Weakness is a fruit of pride, which disguised with poses and words, is really impotence.

The Church has seen in Mary the chatelaine of the nations, the victress of Satan, more powerful than an army in battle array. There in the simplicity of her heart was only one purpose. However indestructible and which not a single tyrant would wound: viz, the purpose to show the glory of Christ. For the conversion of people, and thus an independence of human judgement which stands equal to subjection to God's judgement; a love for neighbor equally great as the sacrifice that brings it along; a challenge of the enemy of God and of the people which unveils a divine fortress in a female heart. Mary continues this service to Jesus and the poor; therefore, she does not stop saying: "Just do what He will tell you."

For Mary the intercession serves to place herself between God and the people. This holds no pretense for sentimental languishing, but a delicate and strong command to obey Jesus, a silent prayer, pure love to obtain graces. And truly all powerful seems here to be the power of Mary's prayer, even if it happens with the scantiness of words which is almost a silence. It reaches namely an infinite result; it changes God's plan to give service to people. More than any other reflection this gives an idea of what kind of position Mary occupies between God and the people. To imitate Mary means to place oneself in that track of humility and love which unites with the Almighty. Hearts which are formed from Marian piety are determined to witness the Gospel, to serve the Church, to saturate society with the wine which makes her drunk of the Holy Spirit. Only like this, water changes into wine; which afterwards, by a still greater miracle, will change into blood, into the blood of God.

Bernard teaches us that God has willed that we would receive everything from the hands of Mary — Mary, Mother of grace and mercifulness. One could say: but the mediator of all grace is Jesus, but Jesus is our brother, our flesh, which He has become through Mary; and to turn oneself to Him via Mary is to place the Mother between Him who is offended and us who are offending. Thus a chain starts, in which Mary listens to the sinner, Jesus listens to Mary and the Father listens to Jesus; and in this relation circulates the Holy Spirit. Jesus comes to us via Mary; we go to Jesus via the same way, as a river bed through which the life of God streams to the people and from the people returns to God. A thought which also Silvio Pellico has translated in verse: "Virginal Consolatrix, hope of the heavily afflicted, you are our mother and also are you the mother of the Saviour!" And thus becomes that living together through Mary the familiar circle in which the life of God circulates.

During the Second Vatican Council, especially during the third session, with respect to ecumenicity, they tried to distinguish clearly the veneration we owe Mary from every form of superstition, of sensitivity or even of Mario Latry. In this connection, the dogmatic constitution of the Church, *Lumen Gentium* states: "Only one is our mediator, Jesus Christ; the maternal task of Mary toward men, in no way obscures or diminishes this unique mediation of Christ, but rather shows His power. On account of her love shown through the ages the Holy Virgin is invoked by the Church under the titles of Advocate, Helper, Assistant and Mediatrix. This is thus to be understood: that nothing is taken away, nothing is added to the dignity and efficacy of Christ, the only mediator." So, the fame of the parents and especially of the mothers, lies in the glorification of their children.

The Church writers from old times describe the relation with a simple analogy by which they present Jesus as the sun and Mary as the moon. If, as Hieronymus says, Mary means the illuminated, then she spreads like the moon, the light which she receives from the sun, Jesus; she spreads the gifts which come from the Father of all light, God. Mary gives the earth the light of Heaven and that is a light which beams from love. For this reason, she is invoked as "shining porch of the light." Mary is the star which leads to Bethlehem. To the generation of the divine life on earth: to follow her is going directly on the way to Christ through the darkness and obstacles of the night. The fact that God loves and crowns the humility, love and devotion of Mary expresses the grandeur of God and discloses the power of Christ, who through integrating with His person the divine into mankind wins this back for God and makes her participating in the divine graces. If this integration elevates the people and at the head of all the most Holy Virgin, then she does not decrease anything from the endless generosity of the Lord, but she elevates and enlightens Him. Mary makes God's glory only greater — Magnificat!

The eternal king, the creator of Heaven and earth, all powerful and sovereign Lord is imprisoned in the Immaculate purity, in the innocent "nothing" of Mary. It is impossible for God to refuse Mary anything and it is impossible for Mary — as she is Mother — to reject anyone who takes his refuge in her. This is a mystery of love, which can only be understood by love. Only when we look to Mary with the eyes of God and that is with the eyes of love, that we then understand the omnipotence of Mary.

We can presume something of the beauty and purity of Mary, as God sees it, from the vision in which Mary shows herself in her magnificence:

> Mary is entirely dressed in white; a dress closed round
> the neck that runs down in loose folds over the breast
> and scrupulously modulates Mary's shapes. The sleeves
> are rather tight and hang down on the pulses. Round
> the middle a girdle keeps the dress together. It is not

made of gold or silver. It seems to be a cord of silk of even color and gloss as the dress. There are no fringes on it and it hangs further down the dress. It only girds up. The head is covered with the same light material as the dress; she is not veiled, but it hangs down along Mary's cheeks and reaches the neck as if forced to it through a fastening. Nevertheless, an oblong fastening, as Mary's white neck is visible. In short, a turban hangs down over the shoulders along the arms and hips to the ground.

The beauty of that white and simple dress is beyond words. The snow is grey and dark compared with it and the lily less beautiful. The whiteness of the material sparkles so much as if she changes into silver. Oh! words are inadequate to describe it! Only in Heaven such a material can exist to clothe Mary, a material of phosphorescent whiteness like a diamond, pearl and opal. It is a gem without being a gem and has to have the splendor of all jewels together to sparkle in such a way! The face of Mary is more round than oval. It has a tint of ivory as certain leaves of the magnolia, and only the lips and the nice light-dark eyebrows bring color to the flowery face. The eyes, not entirely open but half-covered by the eyelids, have the same look as the Son; her eyes have the same sky-blue color as those of Jesus, but a bit lighter of tint. Humanly compared, the eyes of Jesus have the color of sapphire and those of Mary are turquoise.

The serious and sad look of Jesus is also present with Mary, but is blended with a smile: the benign smile of someone who is sad, but yet wants to console and encourage. The hair has the color of ripe grain unless you prefer a golden ducat, yet it tends towards fair-red, more fair than red, while the hair of Jesus tends more towards copper-blond. The long and beautiful hands, with very long and pointed fingers, and delicate white pulses protrude from the narrow sleeves. They are exactly two magnolia leaflets folded in prayer. They give the impression that they have to smell like flowers so much do they resemble flowers in the bud.

She wears not a single necklace. Everything is just Mary, jewel of brilliant alabaster or, better said, of opal, which is illuminated by a flame from the inside. Her glorified body radiates light, a mild light that makes one think of a fiery burning sanctuary lamp before the tabernacle: a lamp of pure alabaster. The feet cannot be seen because the long dress hides them. To behold her does not need any other words. She is the masterpiece of God, the paradise of God and this beauty, which brings about an ecstatic joy and emotion, reveals the beauty of the purity, the power of her prayer and the reverent silence in which God lives. The sight of Mary lets one also understand that we have to see in our enemies also her children. Because, also, for them she has given her Son and accepted them as her children. It makes her sad if we look at them with resentment; then we do not imitate her, who with pitiful love has looked down on the crucifiers of her Son and those who pierced her Immaculate heart.

The power of Mary can only be understood through and from love. The power of Mary is itself a power of love. Everything Mary asks of God is given to her by means of love. Mary is the mother and she can do nothing but love her children. Mary is the endless loving one, the woman whose heart was pierced through by a sword of sorrows, but through which love was not extinguished. Mary, in her endless humility gives God sheer joy by being such a pure creature. By having a heart that only lives for and from love. By having an Immaculate Heart, the masterpiece of His creation. Mary is all the beauty of creation put together. All created love together, all generosity and justice together are not able to even approach the love and purity of Mary. Mary is an endless prayer, a prayer of a creature which is the only one able to give God the honor which is due to Him. In and through Mary, creation finds its justification in the eyes of God. Her life on earth was a perfect "yes" to God and, also, in the glory of Heaven is

Mary nothing else than praise and prayer before the infinite majesty and goodness of God.

In Medjugorje, Mary says that she has come to ask people to pray. "Every new day is for me a prayer attitude. Start everyday with the morning prayer." Mary wants us to learn praying; to learn letting our life become an adoration of the most Holy Trinity. She is our great Advocate, but she needs our prayers in order that she can present them to God. That is her task and her power. God can refuse nothing and Mary, in her motherly love, begs the people for their prayers and sacrifices, so that she can present them to her Son. Mary is an eternal ecstasy of adoration full of reverence. She looks at the Father, silent but with a look of adoration, prayer and hymn. Her posture is a posture of deep reverence and respect. Her love alone already says a wordless "Sanctus" — adore thee.

Full of endless love she gazes at Jesus with a smile which is an endearment. Rich caress from her sweet eyes speaks "I love thee." Her look receives Him in her lap and embraces Him still more dearly in her motherly arms as during His childhood and at His death. Mary amuses herself in contemplation of the Father and the Son. Her face raises itself again and again to look for the love that sparkles high and vertically above her. She receives in an ongoing new embrace the kiss of love and she inclines in her humility, purity and love to return the endearment to the endearment and to say: "Behold, here I am. Your bride, I love you and belong to you. I am yours for eternity" and the Holy Ghost sparkles still more, when Mary's gaze attaches itself to His sparkling. Mary as treasurer of the love distributes the love. Mary in her glory is as it were elected by the Holy Ghost to collect all love in her and to bring these to the Father and the Son, so that the three amalgamate and become one. Mary, elected seat of love, whose smallest wish is a command from God. She is our Advocate before God and what an infinite richness, what an immense gift we have received from God in Mary.

We close this chapter about Mary Advocate with the words of someone who has become famous for having the gift to touch countless simple people and to bring them to God: the Cure d'Ars, Jean Marie Vianney. What we have seen in mystical visions of many great saints, he explains in "simple" words: "The Father eagerly considers the heart of the most Holy Virgin Mary as the masterpiece of His hands. The Son eagerly sees the heart of his mother, the source from which he has drawn the blood which has redeemed us; the Holy Ghost considers it as his temple."

The prophets proclaimed the glory of Mary already before her birth: they compared her with the sun. Indeed, we could compare the apparition of the Holy Virgin with the appearance of a beautiful sunbeam on a misty day. Before she came, the wrath of God hung above our heads as a sword that was ready to pierce us. As soon as the Holy Virgin appeared on earth, His wrath calmed down... She did not know that she would one day become the mother of God. The Holy Virgin has given us life twice: in the incarnation and at the foot of the cross. She is, therefore, twice our mother, but she is still much better than the best mother, because the best mother punishes her child now and then when it is troublesome and beats it even; she thinks that it is beneficial. But the Holy Virgin does not act like that. She is so good, that she treats us with love and never punishes us. The heart of this good mother is all love and mercy: she wants to see us only but happy. To be heard, we need only to turn ourselves towards her. The Son has His justice, the mother has nothing but her love. God loves us so much, that He has died for us. But in the heart of the most Holy Virgin there is only mercy.

If the Son would be on the point of punishing a sinner, Mary would come in between, withhold the sword and beg for grace for the evil-doer. "Mother," our Lord says to her, "I cannot refuse you anything. If hell could be sorry, you would still get his forgiveness." The most Holy Virgin places herself between her Son and us. The greater sinners we are, the more tenderness and pity she feels for us. The child that has given his mother most tears, is dearest to her. Does the mother not always hurry to help the weakest and the one who is most in danger? Does the doctor in the hospital not pay the most attention to those who are seriously sick? The heart of Mary is so full of love for us, that the hearts of all mothers together look like a cube of ice compared with that of hers. Just look how the Holy Virgin is! Her great servant, St.Bernard, often said to her: "I greet thee, Mary." One day this good mother answered him: "I greet you, my son Bernard." The "Hail Mary" is a prayer that never tires. The veneration of the Holy Virgin is glorious and it gives you strength.

When we talk about earthly things or about politics, we soon get bored, but when we talk about the Holy Virgin, it is always refreshing. All saints have a great veneration for our mother; no grace comes from Heaven without having gone through her hands. We cannot enter a house without a talk with the gatekeepers; well then, the Holy Virgin is the gatekeeper of Heaven. If we have to present something to an important person, then we let it be given by someone whom he most likes, so that the mark of honor will be pleasing to him. Thus, our prayers will have a different kind of merit, when they are presented through the Blessed Virgin, as she is the only creature that has never offended God. Only the Blessed Virgin has kept the First Commandment — to adore God alone and love Him above all else. She obeyed this completely.

Everything which the Son asks the Father is given to Him. Everything which the mother asks her Son is given to her in the same way. When we have had something in our hands that smells strongly, it will affect everything with the same smell which we touch; let our prayers go through the hands of the Blessed Virgin; she will let them give forth fragrance. I think that at the end of the world the Blessed Virgin will have peace; but as long as the world still exists, we drag her in all directions ... the Holy Virgin is like a mother with a mass of children — she always runs from one to the other.

Mary remains our Advocate as long as the world lasts.

CHAPTER 5

THE MESSAGES OF THE LADY

Fifty-sixth message, May 31, 1959

I saw as if the sky was torn apart — it really was a tearing apart of the sky! Then I suddenly saw, in all her glory — the Lady! I cannot possibly describe this heavenly, powerful, splendid sight. Never before had I seen her like that. I saw no sheep, globe or cross, only the Lady, but with rays of dazzling glory about her! Then, I suddenly looked at her head and I saw that she wore a crown that I had never seen before. I saw no gold or diamonds, yet I knew very well that it was a crown for it sparkled with light all around, more brilliant than the rarest diamonds. The Lady herself was one blaze of light. Again — it was heavenly, glorious! I cannot explain myself better.

Then below this splendid view I saw a piece of thin, blue sky and underneath, the upperside of the globe. This was completely black. Then I saw the Lady moving her finger from side to side and shaking her head as if in disapproval and warning at the blackness of the world and I heard her say: "Do penance." Then, I saw something very strange. From that dark, black globe there emerged a great variety of human heads. It looked as if they were slowly moving higher until they all at once stood on the half round globe. I examined them, thinking "I never knew that there were so many races and divisions of men." Then I saw the Lady extending her hands in blessing over these people and she no longer looked quite so sad. I heard her say: "Make reparation to Him."

Suddenly the Lady had gone. In her stead I saw a big host. It was exceedingly large and so I could see quite well that it was a normal host, one like those we see in Church, a wafer. Then in front of the host there appeared a chalice. I saw that the chalice was of splendid gold. It toppled over, facing me. Then I saw flowing from this chalice thick streams of blood. All this blood poured upon the globe and spilled over the earth; it was a distressing sight. I began to feel quite sick, all the time streams and streams of blood! This went on for quite a while then the scene suddenly changed and all of it became a brilliant, dazzling Sacred Host. It shone so brightly that I shaded my eyes so as not to get blinded, but I was forced to keep looking at it. The host seemed to be made of white fire. In the center of it was a little opening of depth. I cannot describe it any better. Then, all of a sudden, the host seemed to burst open and exposed to my view was a figure, soaring in mid-air, a person, exceedingly mighty and strong.

Forgive me, please, I cannot convey the strength and majesty this person embodied. It was too overwhelming. I hardly dared to look. I saw one person, but the thought kept recurring in my mind, "and yet there are two;" and then when I looked I saw only one. Still my mind kept repeating "and yet they are two."

All at once there came from the two an indescribable light and in it I saw, breaking out from the center — I cannot express it otherwise — a dove! It shot like an arrow down to the earth, unspeakably bright and I covered my eyes again so as not to go blind. My eyes hurt me and yet again I was forced to keep them open and look at the vision! What a splendor, what a magnificence! The soaring figure, majestic, powerful, grand; and the world now all bathed in light from the radiant dove! And a voice rang out, "He who eats and drinks

Me, receives life eternal and the true Spirit." When I had gazed at all this for a while, the Lady came back again, arrayed in her former glory, exactly as at the beginning. Now, however, I clearly saw the difference between magnificence, if I may say so and the grandeur and majesty of the soaring figure. . Now the Lady looked happy and I heard her say very softly in the distance: "Goodbye." This made me very sad, so that I began to weep for I saw everything slowly fading from my sight.

The messages of the Lady are of a beauty and majesty beyond compare. The apparitions of the Lady in Amsterdam surpass all other apparitions of Mary in their heavenly beauty and expressiveness. It is not only the statues, which express such an emotional and majestic beauty but also the messages themselves, their depth and the definitive character, which almost forces one to an adoring respect. Mary lets herself been seen and known as the Lady of all Nations, the final title, which she has received from God, in order to bring together the nations under the dominion of her Son, Jesus Christ, in the position as Mother of humanity. To her it is given to bring redemption and peace to the world. She is the one who will definitely crush the head of Satan.

This final message of Mary is the keystone and crowning of all Marian apparitions of the last one and one half centuries. It is here, that she asks the Church to acknowledge her officially as the Co-Redemptrix, Mediatrix and Advocate and she promises that she will triumph under this title. The messages of the Lady are in complete accordance with the apocalyptical time, the end of time, in which we live and which are described in Chapter One. In this last chapter we give some of the messages of the Lady which are related to the end of time and the dogma.

Many messages are about the deterioration in which our world exists and the disasters which are the consequences of it.

April 4, 1954:

Then the Lady looks in front of her earnestly and it is as though I see heavy clouds surging around the globe on which she stands. While the globe is rotating fast the Lady points at the globe and says very sadly: "Look to the world — mark well what I am going to tell you." At this, the Lady holds up her right hand and lets me look into it. I see in it a large die and the Lady moves her hand as though shaking it over the world ... then she says "Satan's hand goes all over the world, holding a die. Do you know, Church — community — what this means? Satan is still the prince of this world. He keeps his grasp on everything he can."

May 31, 1954

"The world is encompassed by a false spirit, Satan."

May 31, 1955

"How thoroughly Satan holds the world in his clutches — God knows. He now sends to you to all the nations, His Mother, the Lady of all Nations. She will vanquish Satan, as has been foretold. She will place her foot upon Satan's head."

The messages of the Lady which are related to the dominion of Satan over the world agree with other messages and apparitions which have been given from Rue du Bac, up to our days. In 1982 in Medjugorie, Mary said to Mirjana, one of the visionaries: "You should know that Satan exists. One day he appeared before the throne of God and asked for permission to test the Church during a certain period. God has allowed him to test her during one century. This century is under the power of the Devil, but when the secrets which are entrusted to you have been realized, his power will be destroyed. Already he has started to lose his power and has become aggressive; he destroys marriages, encourages divisions among the priests and causes fallacies and murders."

The dominion of Satan is not only operative in the world, but also present in the Church. The Lady predicts the consequences of this dominion — economical, spiritual and material crises, apostasy, confusion, chaos, fear, corruption, battle, rebellion and disasters.

December 26, 1947

There will come disasters from north to south and from south to west and from west to east. Around and near Jerusalem there will be heavy battles waged. The world, as it were, will be torn into two. There will be much suffering and misery. Economic warfare, boycotting, exchanging rates, disasters. Then I am aware of terrible diseases, cholera and so on. Then tiny little black things are floating around me. I cannot distinguish them with my eyes and it is as if I were made to look at them through something (a microscope) and now I see (what the seeress now knows to be) slides of extraordinary brilliance and upon them those little things enlarged. I do not know how I am to interpret this. "Bacilli"? I ask. Then the Lady says, "It is hellish!" I feel my face swelling and it is swollen when I touch it. It is all bloated and quite stiff. I can no longer move. Then I hear the Lady again, saying "Just think this is what they are trying to find out," and then very softly, "Russia, but the others as well." Finally, the Lady says, "Nations, be warned" and now the Lady disappears.

October 1, 1949

Then suddenly I see the Balkans. There is war. They are fighting again. The Lady says, "Child, there will be a fierce struggle. We have not seen the end of this struggle yet. Economic disasters will come. The empire of England is tottering."

September 20, 1951

Now the Lady looks around her and then at the world. Then I see black patches appear here and there. The Lady says to me, "These are the economic and material disasters that will strike the world. I have said: Disasters will come, disasters of nature. Now I say to you: All these

black patches you see there, are disasters yet to come.
And now I do not only speak of catastrophes of nature."

November 15, 1951

"The world is degenerating. The world is being afflicted
with disaster upon disaster. The world will be and is
economically and materially at a dead end. Wars will
continue until the True Spirit comes with his help."

As remedy against the degeneration and self-destruction of the
world, the Lady gives two gifts, which include a mission at the
same time. The first gift is a prayer. It is a prayer which excels in
simplicity, directness and, at the same time, a theological depth.
The prayer was given on the 11th of February, 1951 and reads "Lord
Jesus Christ, Son of the Father, send now Your Spirit over the earth.
Let the Holy Spirit live in the hearts of all Nations, that they may
be preserved from degeneration, disaster and war. May the Lady of
all Nations, who once was Mary, be our Advocate, Amen."

The prayer excels in its theological depth. It starts with invok-
ing Jesus Christ, our sole Mediator, who is the Son of the Father, to
send His Spirit. Here the whole purpose of all the messages is indicated: The glorification of the divine Trinity. The Lady often speaks
about this expressly.

December 31, 1951

"Now I stand as Advocate in these anxious times. All of
you, 'whoever or whatever' you may be, ask the True
Holy Spirit to descend. You shall beg this of the Father
and the Son. The Blessed Trinity will reign over the
world again."

February 17, 1952

"The Church is the community of nations who are to
adore and worship their Lord and Creator, the Father,
the Son and the Holy Spirit."

May 31, 1955

"Nations, let yourselves not being deceived by false prophets, listen only to Him, to God, the Father, the Son and the Holy Spirit. For the same Father is the same Son [this was said very slowly] the same Father and Son is the same Holy Spirit."

That the prayer starts with the invocation of the Trinity also shows immediately the Advocacy of Mary.

She is not there for herself. She intercedes for mankind as Mother before God for Whom all creation lives.

Then follows the supplication for the Holy Spirit. The Lady explains the necessity of this in different messages.

April 29, 1951

"For the world is not saved by force, the world will be saved by the Spirit."

December 8, 1952

After another thoughtful silence the Lady says: "You must realize why I come as the Lady of all Nations. I come in order to rally all nations in the Spirit, in the Spirit of Truth. All men must learn to find the Holy Spirit. Strive after justice, truth and love. Do not reject your brothers, lead them on to the knowledge of the true spirit."

May 31, 1955

"I will comfort you. Nations, your Mother knows what life is like; your Mother is familiar with sorrow. Your Mother knows what the cross means. Whatever you suffer in this life, your Mother, the Lady of all Nations, suffered before you. She has shown you the way in her own person." The Lady waits a moment and adds very slowly: "But she went up to the Father. She returned to her Son. You too, nations, go to the Father along the way of the cross; you too go to the Son along the same way of the cross; the Holy Spirit will help you to do this. Implore Him now. I cannot repeat this often enough to the world. Have recourse to the Holy Spirit *now*." [The Lady said this very slowly stressing every word.]

After the request to send the Holy Spirit an explanation follows: Let the Holy Spirit live in the hearts of all nations. With this prayer the universal character of Christ's sacrifice is confirmed. Jesus has come for all people. He has carried the sins of all people and He has also given the Spirit for all people. The Lady asks to pray for a new outpouring of the Holy Spirit, a new Pentecost Miracle, but now with a universal character. This new Pentecost miracle, that will come, is a promise, which has been given by Jesus and Mary on several occasions. The new epoch will be an epoch of the Holy Spirit. That the Holy Spirit will be given to all people agrees with the fact, that with God there is no preference between persons.

In Medjugorje, Mary says: "The Muslims, the Orthodox and also the Catholics are equal for my Son and Me: You all are my children. Surely, all religions are not the same, but all people are equal before God, as St.Paul says. It is not sufficient to belong to the Catholic Church in order to be saved. You have to keep the commandments of God and to follow your conscience. Those who are not Catholic, remain all the same creatures, which have been created in God's image and destined to come together one day in the house of the Father. Only those who reject God knowingly will be condemned. To whom little has been given, little will be asked. To whom much has been given (the Catholics), much will be asked. Only God determines the degree of responsibility of His infinite justice and pronounces the judgement." The same spirit is proclaimed from the message of the Lady.

November 15, 1951

Now I am speaking to the whole world when I say: "Nations, whoever or whatever you may be, turn to your

Creator with all your needs. Oh, learn to find Him wherever you are. Ask the Lady of All Nations to be your Advocate."

April 6, 1952

"You, people, whoever or whatever you may be, support and help one another. In the first and most important Commandment (love) you will find everything you are in need of."

March 20, 1953

I see the Lady of All Nations standing before me. She says: "Tell them that the time has now come. It is upon us — the time, when the world will know that I have come as the 'Lady of All Nations.' I wish that now to be made known to the world."

The fact that Mary makes herself known as the "Lady of All Nations" does not mean that she does not respect the special place and vocation of the Catholic Church. On the contrary, she confirms that the Catholic Church as such has to proclaim her. The Pope as Vicar of Christ has herein to fulfill a special role and an important task waits him in connection with the messages of the Lady.

November 15, 1951

Then She continues: "Christians, know your duty! Now I am addressing the Church of Rome and I say to the Pope: 'See that all your subjects know how to bring back the charity of Jesus Christ to this world — this degenerate world.' The Church of Rome must fulfill this precept to the utmost of its power. And then I say, be broadminded, try to establish yourself in this modern world with Jesus Christ on the cross. Study to understand these words fully and carry them into effect. This world can be saved only through the Church that holds this doctrine."

March 19, 1952

I see the Lady of All Nations standing before me. She says: "Tell the Holy Father that the Lady of All Nations will give him his sign. The Church, 'Rome' will have to face a terrible struggle. Before the year 2000 much will have changed in the Church, the community. Nevertheless, the substance will remain."

October 11, 1953

For a long time the Lady stands silent and then resumes: "The Lady of All Nations has the power to bring the world peace. Yes, she has to be asked for it under this title. The Lady of All Nations will assist the Church of Rome. The Church of Rome — the community — should invoke Mary, the Mother of the Lord Jesus Christ, under this new title: The 'Lady of All Nations.' They should say My prayer against degeneration, disaster and war and spread it among all peoples. I shall help the Church of Rome — the community. The nations should call on me under this title."

March 20, 1953

Then the Lady, very slowly and distinctly adds, "And now the Lady of All Nations promises to grant true peace to all nations. But the nations — together with the Church — understand well — together with the Church, will have to say my prayer in this year. Inform the Sacristan. Tell him that *now* the time has come. Great world events are still to come."

The urgent reasons why we have to pray for the Holy Spirit is that the nations may be preserved from degeneration, disaster and war. Only the Holy Spirit can make the world one, can bring peace between the peoples. The disasters, also disasters of nature, are the consequences of the degeneration of mankind. Over and over again the Lady speaks about it.

June 9, 1946

The Lady looks sadly on mankind and says very deject-
edly: "Righteousness, truth and love are not to be found
among men." After that the Lady, gazing intently in front
of her says: "Disaster upon disaster! For a second time
I tell you: As long as these are missing, there can be no
true peace."

Then the Lady says: "By praying and not only by
praying, but especially by working for the right end ...
work and watch!" Then I notice that the Lady has stepped
aside and from the other direction demons are coming
towards me.

I hear the Lady say: "I predict another great catas-
trophe for the world." This she says very sadly and she
keeps on making gestures of warning. She continues:
"If people would only listen!" and she keeps shaking
her head, "But they will not!" Then I sense a short span
of time and hear: "Apparently things go well for a short
time." I see the globe and the Lady points to it and it
looks as though the globe will burst asunder on all sides.

May 7, 1949

Suddenly I see the Lady sitting in front of me, clad in
mourning, with a white veil draped over her head. She
looks very old. She sits stooped. The Lady says: "We
are here in the darkness; it is the degeneration in mankind." Then I see a crucifix before me and the body slides
down from it, so that the wood is left bare. "The way of
the cross begins anew," the Lady says. I see deep fur-
rows in her face and big tears running down the cheeks
of the Lady.

Then the Lady says: "Nature too will change!" I
hear the words: "Christ is gone." I go about looking for
Him and I hear: "Realism, a spirit of realism." I also see
this spirit in some way or other.

February 11, 1951

Then the Lady says again to me: "There will be again a great natural disaster coming. The great ones of this world will not agree. The people will seek here and there. Think about the false prophets. Seek and ask only about the true Holy Spirit. For it is, at the moment, a war of ideas. The battle is not anymore about races and nations, the battle is about the spirit. Understand this well."

June 15, 1952

"This present time is the time of the Holy Spirit. All of you must ask the Holy Spirit to make His truth prevail over the world.

"Moral decline prevails in the world at the moment. People in higher positions only strive after power; people in higher positions think only of material things; people are being bewildered and led in the wrong direction." Then the Lady points at the globe and says: "Just look at all those countries! Nowhere is unity to be found, nowhere peace, nowhere repose for the nations. Everywhere there is tension, everywhere anxiety. The Lord Jesus Christ lets this be. His time will come. There will be an intervening period of unrest — caused by humanism, paganism, godlessness, snakes. These will attempt to control the world."

May 31, 1955

"You will have to endure a great deal as yet in this century. You, nations of this area, do you realize that you are under the protection of the Lady of All Nations; call upon her as the Advocate; ask her to stave off all disasters; ask her to banish degeneration from this world. Degeneration breeds disaster. Degeneration generates war."

The last sentence of the prayer is a request, that the Lady of All Nations may be our Advocate. As Mary has always been Advocate for the people before the Son and the Father, she is that now especially under the title of the "Lady of All Nations." It is a special grace, a special gift from God, that He now sends Mary to the world in this capacity. Under this title may she bring grace, peace and redemption. She is the Mother, the Lady to whom all nations can turn for her powerful intercession. The Lady herself stresses this.

March 4, 1951

Now the Lady stands motionless in front of me and I have a clear view of her. Then she says: "Now I will explain to you why I have come in this way: I am the Lady standing in front of the cross. My head, hands and feet are like those of a human being. The trunk, however, belongs to the Spirit, because the Son came through the Will of the Father. Now, however, the Spirit is to descend upon the world and this is why I want people to pray for His coming." Then the Lady pauses before she adds: "I am standing upon the globe because this message concerns the whole world."

Then the Lady seems to draw a semi-circle with her hand, while she says: "Look closely." Now I see a semi-circle stretching from one crossbeam to the other. The semi-circle seems to consist of a peculiar light and in it I see appear letters printed in black. On the left side I see the words: "the Lady," in the middle above "of all" and at right "Nations." Then the Lady says again: "I have my special reasons for giving you this here [in Germany]. What they are you will learn later. You have my message of today. Pass on everything with great care. The spirit of untruth is making such appalling progress that it is necessary to act quickly. The whole world is degenerating and for this reason the Son sends the Lady of All Nations, who once was Mary."

April 15, 1951

Once again the Lady shows herself clearly in front of the cross and says: "Listen well and be sure to grasp what I am going to explain to you. But first I repeat, the Son came into the world as the Redeemer of mankind. The work of redemption was the cross. He was sent by the Father. Now, however, the Father and the Son want to send the 'Lady' throughout the whole world. In the past, too, she went before the Son and followed Him. For this reason I am now standing on the world, on the globe. The cross stands firmly fixed, implanted in it."

April 29, 1951

Then, coming still closer, the Lady resumes: "Now you see me standing here clearly, very clearly. This is the way the picture should be made known throughout the world. My child, insist upon it that these things are carried out. They should not hesitate; they should act. The situation is far too serious. Nobody realizes just how serious. I also wish to be made known to those people who are being kept away from the Son. Do save the people who are forced to turn away from Him. You are duty bound to do so. The world is degenerating, so badly, that it was necessary for the Father and the Son to send me into the world, among all the peoples in order to be their Advocate and to save them."

In the prayer itself it is confirmed that the Lady of All Nations is the same Mary, the Mother of Jesus. Also, about this, the Lady gives some explanations in her messages.

July 2, 1951

"'Who once was Mary' means: many people have known Mary just as Mary. Now, however, in the new era, which is beginning now, I wish to be the Lady of All Nations. Everyone will understand this."

April 6, 1952

The Lady is here again! She says: "Now you must listen and transmit carefully what I have come to say today. Tell the theologians that I am not pleased about their alterations of the prayer. May the Lady of All Nations, who once was Mary, be our Advocate — that must remain as it is. This time is our time. Pass on the following to the theologians: 'The Lady came with the sacrifice of the cross: The Son said to His Mother: Woman, behold thy Son.' So you see it was at the sacrifice of the cross that the change came about."

The Lord and Master chose Miriam or Mary from among all the women, to become the "Mother" of His Divine Son! At the sacrifice of the cross, however, she became the Lady ("Woman") — the Co-Redemptrix and Mediatrix. This was announced by the Son at the time that He returned to His Father.

The prayer in its simplicity and directness is a summary of the germ of the faith. It has a theological structure which is in complete accordance with Catholic tradition, as given in Chapters 2 up to and including Chapter 4. The prayer starts with an invocation of Jesus, our sole Mediator with the Father; next, an indication of Jesus: Son of the Father. The glorification of the Father had always been the purpose of Jesus during His life and it is also our vocation to glorify the Father; then, a prayer for the Holy Spirit, Who is given to us through Jesus and in Whom we are only able to live as God's children. The prayer that the Holy Spirit may live in the hearts of all people, so that they remain preserved from degeneration, disaster and war, is a prayer for the coming of God's kingdom and shows, at the same time, how much God is concerned about the actual situation of mankind. Salvation-history comes about in the history of mankind and considering the state of degeneration of the world, it is now more than ever necessary that the kingdom of God is broken through by the Holy Spirit.

The hour of Christ's return is near and all signs in our world indicate this. The prayer that the Lady of All Nations, who once was Mary, may be our Advocate confirms the place which Mary has received from God in His eternal plan of salvation. In a nutshell, but with a heavenly beauty and expressiveness, the prayer lets us feel what its meaning is.

Perhaps still more important than the prayer — though in the messages from Heaven everything is of eternal importance and thus the difference is a bit artificial — is the dogma which Mary announces. To speak about a new dogma could seem to be absurd in a time in which it seems as if people have nothing but dislike for dogmas and a dogmatic faith. We can only understand this when we, enlightened by the Holy Spirit, understand something of the heavenly logic. This logic lets us simultaneously see the importance of the announced dogma and the prediction of the big battle which will arise about it. Because of the importance of this part of the Lady's messages, we will give many quotations.

April 15, 1951

The Lady is pointing to the girdle around her waist for this is what she wants me to look at. Then the Lady speaks again: "You have reported everything correctly. You are on the right path. Only, have another look at this cloth."

And then it would seem that the Lady removes the girdle from her waist to show me how she puts it on — she wraps it round herself once and then a second time. She tucks in the end of the two layered cloth on her left side, leaving one small end hanging down.

"Mark well, what this means," says the Lady. "This represents the loin cloth of the Son. For I stand as the Lady in front of the cross of the Son. This picture will precede [and the Lady repeats 'Will Precede'] a dogma, a new dogma. Now I will explain it to you. So listen carefully."

"The Son came into the world as the Redeemer of men and the work of redemption was the cross, with all its sufferings both of body and spirit."

"But first I repeat: The Son came into the world as the Redeemer of mankind. The work of redemption was the cross. He was sent by the Father. Now, however, the Father and the Son want to send the 'Lady' throughout the whole world. In the past, too, she went before the Son and followed Him. For this reason I am now standing on the world, on the globe."

Now the Lady comes to stand in front of it, as the Son's Mother, who with Him has accomplished this work of redemption. This picture speaks clearly and now is the time to bring it into the world, for the world is once more in need of the cross. The Lady, however, really stands here as the Co-Redemptrix and Advocate. About this, much controversy will arise.

April 29, 1951

"Repeat this after me: 'The new dogma will be: the *dogma of the Co-Redemptrix.*' Notice I lay special emphasis on *Co.* I have said that it will arouse much controversy.

"For the Father, the Son and the Holy Spirit will to send the Lady, chosen to bear the Redeemer, into THIS world, as Co-Redemptrix and Advocate. I have said, 'This time is our time.' By this I mean the following: The world is caught up in degeneration and superficiality. It is at a loss, therefore, the Father sends me to be the Advocate, to implore the Holy Spirit to come."

"In the suffering, both spiritual and bodily, the Lady, the Mother, has shared; She has always gone before. As soon as the Father had elected her, she was the Co-Redemptrix with the Redeemer, who came into the world as the Man-God. Tell that to your theologians. I know well, the struggle will be hard and bitter [and then the Lady smiles to herself and seems to gaze into the far distance], but the outcome is already assured."

May 31, 1951

The Lady is here again and she says: "I am here and have come to tell you that I wish to be 'Mary — the Lady of All Nations.' Look closely, I am standing be- · fore the cross of the Redeemer. My head, my hands and my feet are those of a human being, as those of the Son of man. The rest belongs to the Spirit. My feet are firmly planted upon the globe, for it is the wish of the Father and the Son to send me into the world in these times as the Co-Redemptrix, Mediatrix and Advocate. This will constitute a new and last Marian dogma. This picture will be before it. This dogma will be much disputed and yet it will prevail.

"I have repeated these things to you so that you may once more make them clear to your director and the theologians and be able to refute their objections."

Then the Lady waits a while and looks in front of her and she continues: "Theologians, you should have no difficulty if you consider that the Lord and Master had predestined the Lady for sacrifice. For the sword had already been directed at the heart of the Mother. My meaning is that I have always gone before the Son in spiritual and physical suffering."

July 2, 1951

"Now watch well and listen. The following is the explanation of the new dogma: As Co-Redemptrix, Mediatrix and Advocate I am standing on the globe in front of the cross of the Redeemer. By the will of the Father, the Redeemer came on earth to accomplish this, the Father used the Lady, thus, from the Lady the Redeemer received only — I am stressing the word "only" — flesh and blood, that is to say, the body.

"From my Lord and Master the Redeemer received His Divinity. In this way the Lady became Co-Redemptrix."

August 15, 1951

I see the Lady. She says: "Today I have come as the Lady of All Nations." Then the Lady motions around her and, looking at me, says: "I have crushed the snake with my foot. I have become united to my Son as I had always been united with Him. This is the 'dogma' that has gone before in the history of the Church. As Co-Redemptrix, Mediatrix and Advocate, I stand here, now in this time, in our time, the Dogma of the Assumption had to proceed it. The last and greatest dogma will follow. The sacrifice stands and will stand at the center of the world, in THIS era.

"This is the will of the Father and the Son, with whom I have been wholly reunited. Just as the Son had known me (on earth) so He took me back again. The last Marian dogma — the Lady standing in front of the cross as the Co-Redemptrix in this present time — will be the principal one."

November 15, 1951

"The Lady of All Nations is standing here before the cross of her Son. Her feet are placed on the center of the earth; around her is the flock of Jesus Christ. I come as the Co-Redemptrix — Mediatrix at this time, Co-Redemptrix I was already at the Annunciation." (Now I ask the Lady what this means). "This means that the Mother became Co-Redemptrix by the Will of the Father. Tell your theologians this. Tell them, moreover, that this will be the last dogma in Marian history."

December 31, 1951

Now again the Lady allows me to see her picture clearly. It looks as though she came forward. Then the Lady says: "Transmit the following exactly: the Father, the Lord and Master, has willed the handmaid of the Lord to come into this world as Miriam or Mary. She was chosen from among all women as Co-Redemptrix, Mediatrix and Advocate. Say to your theologians: 'She has been made Co-Redemptrix already at the beginning. This time is our time.'

"The Lady of All Nations stands in the middle of the world in front of the cross. She enters time as Co-Redemptrix, Mediatrix and Advocate. She will pass into Marian history under this title. The new and last dogma in Marian history will be the Dogma of the Co-Redemptrix and Mediatrix. Now I stand as Advocate in these anxious times. The Lady stands here as the Advocate. It is the Creator we are concerned with and not the Lady. Tell this to your theologians."

February 17, 1952

Now the Lady waits in silence for a long time. Then she resumes: "The Lord and Master selected a woman called Miriam or Mary from among all the peoples of the world. She was destined, through the Will of the Father, to bring the Son of man into the world, together with His Church and the cross. The Lady was the handmaid of the Lord. She bore the Son of man through the Will of the Father and was thus necessarily allied with the Church and the cross. This woman stands in front of you in this present time as the Co-Redemptrix, Mediatrix and Advocate. Let the following words sink in well: The (woman or) Lady of All Nations can and will bestow on all the peoples of the world, who have recourse to her — grace, redemption and peace. To you all, however, falls the task of introducing the Lady of All Nations to the whole world."

April 6, 1952

"This time is our time. The forthcoming dogma is the last Marian dogma, namely the Lady of All Nations as the Co-Redemptrix, Mediatrix and Advocate. At the sacrifice of the cross the Son announced this title to the whole world. Whoever or whatever you are, I am for you the 'Lady.'"

June 15, 1952

After this the Lady gazes in front of her for a long time, then she begins to speak again, saying: "The Lady who once was Mary. Only at the departure of the Lord Jesus Christ did co-redemption have its beginning. Only when the Lord Jesus Christ went away, did she become the Mediatrix and Advocate. When departing, the Lord Jesus Christ gave to all the nations the 'Lady of All Nations.' Now the time has come for her to announce this title to the world. Tell your theologians this."

October 5, 1952

"I am here again. I have come to deliver a special message, pass on everything well.

"Never has Miriam or Mary in the community, the Church, been officially called Co-Redemptrix. Never has she officially been called Mediatrix. Never has she officially been called Advocate. These three thoughts are not only closely connected, they form one whole. Therefore, this will be the keystone of Marian history; it will become the Dogma of Co-Redemptrix, Mediatrix and Advocate. I do not reproach the theologians if I say: 'Why can you not come to an agreement about this dogma?'

"Once more I shall explain it and make it clearer still: 'The Father sent the Lord Jesus Christ as the Redeemer of All Nations.' The Lord Jesus Christ was this from the beginning. He became this in the sacrifice and in His going to the Father.

"Miriam or Mary became the handmaid of the Lord. Chosen by the Father and the Holy Spirit. From the beginning she was in virtue of this choice, the Co-

Redemptrix, Mediatrix and Advocate of All Nations. Only at the departure of the God-man, the Lord Jesus Christ, she became the Co-Redemptrix, Mediatrix and Advocate. When leaving, in one final act, the Lord Jesus Christ gave Miriam or Mary to the nations, gave her as the Lady of All Nations.

"He spoke the words: 'Woman, behold thy Son; Son, behold thy Mother — one act!' And by this, Miriam or Mary received this new title.

"How is it that this new title — The Lady of All Nations — only now enters the world? It is because the Lord reserved it for the present time. The other dogmas had to come first; just as her life on earth had to precede the Lady of All Nations. All previous dogmas comprised the life and the departure of the 'Lady.' For the theologians this simple explanation should suffice. It was necessary to give this explanation once more."

December 8, 1952

"My message of today is destined for all nations: I am entering these times as Co-Redemptrix, Mediatrix and Advocate. In one act the Lord gave Mary these three titles — gave these three concepts in one significant act. This new dogma will be much disputed. Therefore, I have given that detailed explanation."

April 4, 1954

I see the Lady standing with a serious look on her face. She says to me: "Once more I am here. Listen well! From the outset the handmaid of the Lord was chosen to be Co-Redemptrix. Tell your theologians that they can find it all in their books!"

The Lady pauses briefly, then smiling to herself, she says, almost in a whisper: "I am not bringing a new doctrine. I am *now* bringing *old* ideas." She waits again and then continues: "Because the Lady is Co-Redemptrix, she is also Mediatrix and Advocate; not only because she is the Mother of the Lord Jesus Christ, but — and mark this well — because she is the Immaculate Conception."

"Theologians, I ask you, do you still have objections to this dogma? You will find these words and ideas. I ask you to work for this dogma. No, fear nothing! There will be a clash. The others indeed will attack you, but the simplicity of this dogma lies in these last thoughts which Mary, the Lady of All Nations, puts before you today. Do fight and ask for this dogma: It is the crowning of your Lady!" (The Lady says this with emphasis on almost every word). Then she gazes in front of her for quite a while with a particular expression on her face, as if she looked into the distance and says: "The Lady, the handmaid of the Lord, was chosen and made fruitful by the Holy Spirit."

The Lady pauses and says very slowly: "The Lady was chosen. She was also present at the Descent of the Holy Spirit. The Holy Spirit had to come down upon the Apostles (and raising her finger she adds with emphasis) — the first theologians! For this reason the Lord willed that His Mother should be present there. His Mother, the Lady of All Nations, became, at the departure of her Son, the Lady of All Nations, the Co-Redemptrix, Mediatrix and Advocate, in the presence of one Apostle, one theologian, to be witness to it. For he had to take care of the "Mother." She had to take care of her "Apostles." Now the Lady looks at me and says with emphasis: "This is the last time that the Lady speaks about this dogma. She will return, but for other matters."

"Tell your theologians, however, that now they have everything in their hands. Now they have to accomplish the will of the Lord Jesus Christ. This dogma must come as a keystone of the Marian thoughts. Tell the theologians that the Lady of All Nations will see to its fulfillment."

For one who understands something of the Catholic Faith, the messages of the Lady are just a confirmation of what always has been understood about Mary by the Fathers of the Church, the Saints and mystics. Indeed, the Lady brings, as she says herself, no new doctrine, but wants an old thought officially to be confirmed.

The novelty of the messages of the Lady is not in her doctrine. The novelty lies in the way in which it is manifested. The messages of the Lady are the most beautiful and impressive of all apparitions and revelations which Mary has given to mankind. And the dogma is nothing else than a theological confirmation of the mysterious and moving beauty in which she shows herself.

The messages and the apparitions of the Lady are indeed of heavenly and incomparable beauty. Mary shows herself as the "Mother," the Lady of All Nations. She does not give special signs. "The signs are in my words," says the Lady. And so it is. The messages themselves give such a dazzling light upon the nature of the Lady and upon our world, that for a good listener, further signs are superfluous. The revelation of the Lady of All Nations lets us experience the immense love which Mary, as a Mother, has for all people. They let us experience something of her Immaculate Heart that as Co-Redemptrix remains beating for every being till the end of time. It is moving how Mary appears to us in the messages of Amsterdam: Her generosity, her concern and compassion, her care for the world and humanity show us her true heart in a superb way. She really is the "Mother," the "Lady" whom Jesus has left behind for us, when He returned to the Father. She really is the Advocate who is acquainted with all the needs of the world and who suffers along with us in a manner which makes us feel her boundless love for us. She really is Co-Redemptrix. She lets us experience the immense love which she has for the Holy Trinity and also teaches us this love. The signs of the Lady of All Nations are in her words. The reading of the messages, of course in the right condition of faith, is redeeming.

Our hearts melt by the warmth, the light and the love which the message spread. They purify our hearts from all irregular love for the things of this world. They unite us with the love which Mary has for Jesus and for all people. They purify our view of the world. They let us see in all clarity the works of Satan: All the inhuman and degenerated situations in which Satan has plunged mankind. They let us experience that Mary crushes the head of Satan. Through the reading of the messages, our own hearts are being filled with gratitude towards the Creator and all darkness is removed. The reading of the messages fills us also with love and concern for mankind and makes us desire the return of Christ and the promised outpouring of the Holy Spirit, which will purify the world and let the nations live in unity and peace.

It is not the Lady of All Nations trying to serve herself. All her messages are aimed to bring back mankind to the Lord Jesus Christ. It is her only aim to prepare the coming of the Holy Spirit, the Spirit of her Son. . It is her only aim to beautify the community — the Church — according to the aim of Jesus. It is her only aim to give the people a foretaste of Heaven, especially of the Eucharist. "The kingdom of Christ is the same as His Eucharistic kingdom," says the Lady. It is her only aim that the first and most important commandment is going to be lived; viz. the love for God and the love for our neighbour. The Lady shows herself in the messages as the Immaculate Mother who only wants salvation and happiness of her children. She reveals herself as the one to whom everybody, whoever or whatever that person may be, can take refuge. She wants nothing else than to make mankind immaculate, beautiful, beaming like a bride who waits for her loved one.

A dogma is a theological translation of a mystery of faith. It exceeds our human mind, but surely it is a striking and even an infallible translation of a secret of God. Mary asks for the dogma of Co-Redemptrix, Mediatrix and Advocate. She surely is this, whether the Church pronounces it or not. But, all the same, Mary asks and predicts this dogma. Not for her glory (she has received this from God), but for the salvation of people. When the Church pronounces this dogma, the people of goodwill will penetrate deeper into the mystery of Mary. It is a mystery of light and love, a mystery of salvation for all mankind. God in His infinite compassion and wisdom has disposed it thus. Let us, therefore, not hesitate and obey whatever Heaven wants. It will mean the beginning of an era of the Holy Spirit, a period of peace and joy for all people.

Our Lady of All Nations Who Once Was Mary

POSTSCRIPT

"Truly, truly, I tell you most solemnly, anyone who does not enter the sheepfold through the gate, but gets in some other way, is a thief and a brigand. The one who enters through the gate is the shepherd of the flock. The gatekeeper let him in, the sheep hear his voice, one by one he calls his own sheep and leads them out. When he has brought out his flock, he goes ahead of them and the sheep follow because they know his voice. They never follow a stranger but run away from him, they do not recognize the voice of a stranger."

Perhaps the most important question which might be asked about this book is the question about what authority might be given to it. With what authority can we speak in this manner about the "end of times" and the meaning of Mary in the salvific plan God?

This question will never be conclusively answered in a rational manner. The answer lies on a different level. It is the same authority with which Jesus spoke and which is recognized by "his sheep who know his voice." The authority of this book is the authority of the Catholic Tradition, in which the Church has recognised and acknowledged the Holy Spirit. All the voices of the saints, mystics and visionaries agree; their voice, though again and again in different words, always has the same sound. It is always the light, the wisdom and the love of God Himself, which illuminates the different views, messages and visions. The authority of this book is similar to the authority which might be given to people like Augustine, Grignion De Monfort, John of the Cross, Bernard,

Maximilian Kolbe and all the other saints and Fathers of the Church from the Catholic Tradition. The authority of this book is similar to the authority that might be given to graceful people like A.C. Emmerich, Maria Valtorta, Sister Faustina, Adriane Von Speyr and many others, who have had private revelations which agree with the Catholic Faith and clarify and deepen it. The authority of this book is similar to the authority of today's charismatic gifted people who have received a special light of the Holy Spirit — and, as such, are also acknowledged by the Church — for the benefit of the Church and mankind; people like Frank Duff, Chiara Lubich, Don Gobbi, Marthe Robin, Vassula Ryden and many others.

Finally, the authority of this book leans on the truth of the many apparitions which have taken place in the last one and one half centuries: Rue de Bac, La Salette, Lourdes, Fatima, Medjugorje, Garabandal, Amsterdam and many others. Many of these apparitions have been acknowledged as credible — though there was no obligation to believe them; others do not have this acknowledgment yet, but breathe the same spirit and bring forth the same fruits of conversion and healing. It is, thus, at least very superficial not to take these apparitions with their messages seriously and to deny all authority to them. The question about the authority of this book is the same question which the Pharisees put to Jesus: "With what authority do you say all these things?" The answer of Jesus was a question in return: "Was the baptism of John the Baptist human or from Heaven? The Pharisees failed to give an answer because they feared the people who held John the Baptist as a prophet. To acknowledge the baptism of John the Baptist, however, as "coming from Heaven" would mean that they would have to acknowledge all authority to the words of Jesus — and this they did not want.

It is the same in our time. The people — especially theologians — are remarkable creatures. They spend a lot of time looking for the "truth." A truth is only then acknowledged as such when nothing logical and rational can be brought against it. The intellect is the final norm for truth. As a consequence, today nothing is acknowledged as "truth," because there is always some thought to be found which can give a nuance to a certain proposition. Only the bare fact that every being has to die is still being accepted as "truth" by most people, because rationally there is not much to be brought against it (though the rising faith in re-incarnation is an attempt to escape this truth).

This fundamental disposition of doubt is sometimes also recommended as a virtue; one is allergic to certainties, absolute truth and last, but not least, to infallibility. The "seeking" itself for truth is valued higher than the finding of truth. They investigate the Gospels with the means of shrewdness, which the human mind can produce, on the way to the "truth."

When the Church, however, — according to the promise of her founder — offers mankind a safe anchor and declares certain truth of faith as sure, then the theologians jump up and do everything in their power to undermine these truths. Logic-wise the dogma of the infallibility itself is the horror of horrors...

I do not want to go any deeper because it is so transparent and at the same time, so repugnant, as it is finally a result of human haughtiness and pride. Indeed, to accept a truth humbly, which arises above the immediate intellectual understanding, requires a renouncing of the human feeling of superiority. It requires that in simplicity one gives his confidence to an "exterior" voice, to the authority of someone else without having that grasp of the intellect regarding the announcement. It is not surprising that places of pilgrimage such as Fatima, Medjugorje, Amsterdam, etc. and messages of Don Gobbi, Marguerite, Vassula Ryden, etc. are scornfully and contemptuously being spoken of by learned and intellectuals and that they feel themselves far above them; they are "religion of the stupid" or "opium for the people."

Apparitions and heavenly messages do not, of course, fall by definition under the grip of the human intellect and thus they are treated as "accidental" or even as negative and undesired religious phenomena. Few theologians engage themselves seriously with the messages from Heaven; it is simply not interesting enough for them. as it does not elevate their respect and prestige. Their "shrewdness" is always smashed up on the sublimity of the light of the Holy Spirit and of Mary's revelations.

From experience I know that God glorifies Himself in the simple faithful who entrust themselves in childlike simplicity and faith to their heavenly Mother and who take the messages seriously. The "learned" have simply no idea of how many graces and mystical gifts God pours into the hearts of numerous simple faithful. It is a small flock which recognizes the voice of Jesus and Mary and follow this voice. They are the "sheep" in whom Jesus and Mary perform their works of charity and compassion. The "wise people of this world" will be made ashamed by these simple people.

A second question regarding this book — and in general regarding the value of apparitions — is the question of how far this really serves the unity of Christians. Is it not true that the heavenly messages and apparitions of Mary are unacceptable for non-Catholics? Besides that, Mary always speaks in her messages about the primacy of "Rome" and she confirms the faith in the Vicarship of Christ by the Pope. How can Mary and the Pope contribute to the unity of Christendom, as the teachings about the papacy and Mary are the greatest obstacles for the unity? A third obstacle is the confirmation which Mary gives everywhere regarding the faith of the Roman Catholic Church in the Eucharist, as Body and Blood of Christ. Can it be still more serious?

In answer to these objections, I'd like to say that it is a complete illusion to think that the unity of the Christians can ever be reached outside the truth. It is Jesus Himself — who is the Truth — who will make the Christians one. But it is also a complete illusion to think that the unity can be reached with disregard to the meaning which Jesus Himself attaches to His Mother, to the Church and to the sacraments. It is absolutely unthinkable that unity can ever be reached when not all Christians acknowledge Mary as their heavenly Mother, when they do not understand the Eucharist as the Body and Blood of Christ, in which He really is present, and when the Pope is not acknowledged as the Vicar of Christ.

All this has nothing to do with "Roman triumphalism;" it is simply the truth; it is simply the revelation Jesus has given to us. Nowadays, it is like this — and in this respect Catholics and non-Catholics are in the same boat — that the doctrines regarding Mary, the Eucharist and the Pope are practically not accepted by anybody. It is for Catholics, perhaps, almost more difficult to accept the simple doctrines of the Church than for the non-Catholics. This is so, as the Catholics have denied and rejected their own treasures, while non-Catholics have, for a great part, less guilt because they have grown up in a different tradition. Catholics should have known better.

The truth about Mary, the Eucharist and the Church are absolute conditions for the unity of Christians, however difficult it can be to accept these truths. To let go these truths means, however, bankruptcy of the whole of Christianity. The promise of Jesus that the gates of hell will not prevail over the Church is, however, the guarantee that this will not happen.

To wind up with this book, we come back once more to the question about the authority it can be given. Ultimately, this authority cannot be "enforced" or shown on purely rational grounds. The authority is, however, the authority of love. Whoever reads and listens to the heart, whoever opens himself as a child for the beauty and the truth of the heavenly messages, understands automatically the authority of Mary, that it is the authority of love. Therefore, we conclude this book with a vision of Maria Valtorta. It is a vision of Jesus' death. From no other vision have I better understood how great the love of Jesus was for His Mother. From no other vision have I understood how true the Dogma of Maria as Co-Redemptrix, Mediatrix and Advocate is, though these theological ideas are not all present in the vision. From no other vision have I understood how much our religion is a religion of love to the very end and how much Mary is the Mother. I hope that every reader puts aside, for a moment, all blockades of reason for this vision, in order to penetrate into that moving spectacle of the moment in which Mary "has earned" the title Queen of Heaven and Earth.

> The suffering becomes ever more intense. The body has the first curves of the neck cramp and every shriek of the people intensifies it. The death of the muscles and of the nerves spreads itself from the tortured members to the trunk and makes the breathing ever more difficult, the contraction of the midriff ever more weaker and the beating of the heart ever more irregular.
>
> The face of Christ passes, in turns, from very deep red blushes to the greenish paleness of a person bleeding to death. His lips move with great difficult because the overstrained nerves of the neck and the head itself, that for dozens of times have acted as a lever for the

whole body, pushing on the cross bar, spread the cramp also to the jaws. His throat, swollen by the obstructed carotid arteries, must be painful and must spread its edema to the tongue, which looks swollen and slow in its movements. His back, even in the moments when the tetanizing contractions do not bend it in a complete arch from the nape of His neck to His hips, leaning at extreme points against the stake of the cross, bends more and more forward, because the limbs are continuously weighed down by the burden of the dead flesh.

The people cannot see this situation very clearly because the light now is like dark ashes and only those who are at the foot of the cross can see well.

At a certain moment, Jesus collapses forwards and downwards, as if He were already dead. He no longer pants, His head hangs inertly forward, His body, from His hips upwards, is completely detached from the cross, forming an angle with its bar.

Mary utters a cry: "He is dead!" A tragic cry that spreads in the dark air and Jesus seems really dead.

Another cry of a woman replies to her and I see a bustle in the group of women. Then some ten people go away holding something, but I cannot see who goes away. The foggy light is too faint. It looks as we are immersed in a cloud of very dense volcanic ash.

"It is not possible," shout some of the priests and the Judeans. "It is a simulation to make us go away. Soldier, prick Him with your lance. It is a good medicine to give His voice back to Him." And as the soldiers do not do so, a volley of stones and clods of earth fly towards the cross, hitting the martyr and falling back on the armor of the Romans.

The medicine, as the Judeans say ironically, works the wonder. Some of the stones have certainly hit the target, perhaps the wound of a hand, or the head itself, because they were aiming high. Jesus moans pitifully and recovers His senses. His thorax begins to breathe again with difficulty and His head moves from left to right, seeking where it may rest in order to suffer less, but finding nothing but greater pain.

With great difficulty, pressing once again on His tortured feet, finding strength in His will, and only in it, Jesus stiffens on the cross. He stands upright, as if He were a healthy man with all His strength. He raises His face, looking with wide open eyes at the world stretched at His feet; at the far away town which one can just see indistinctly as vague whiteness in the mostly dark sky where every trace of blue and of light has disappeared. And to this closed, compact, low sky, resembling a huge slab of dark slate, He shouts in a loud voice, overcoming with His will power and with the need of His soul the obstacle of His swollen tongue and His edematous throat: "Eloi, Eloi, lama sabachthani!" (I hear him say so). He must feel that He is dying, in an absolute abandonment by Heaven, if He confesses His Father's abandonment with such an exclamation.

People laugh and deride Him. They insult Him saying: "God has nothing to do with you! Demons are cursed by God!"

Other people shout: "Let us see whether Elijah, whom He is calling, will come to save Him."

And others say: "Give Him some vinegar, that He may gargle his throat. It helps one's voice! Elijah or God, as it is uncertain what this madman wants, are far away... A loud voice is required to make oneself heard!" And they laugh like hyenas or like demons.

But no soldier gives him vinegar and no one comes from Heaven to give comfort. It is the solitary, totally cruel, also, supernaturally cruel, agony of the Great Victim.

The avalanches of desolate grief, which had already oppressed Him at Gethsemane, come back again. The waves of sins of all the world come back to strike the Shipwrecked Innocent, to submerge Him in their bitterness. And above all what comes back is the sensation, more crucifying than the cross itself, more despairing than any other torture, that God has abandoned Him and that His prayer does not rise to Him. And this is the final torture. The one that accelerates death, because it squeezes the last drops of blood out of the pores, because it crushes the still living remaining fibres of His heart, because it ends what the first knowledge of this abandonment has begun — death. Because this is the very first cause, by which Jesus has died, O God, Who has struck Him for our sake! Because what becomes of a man when deserted by You through Your abandonment? Either insane or dead. Jesus could not become insane, because His intelligence was divine and since intelligence is spiritual, it triumphed over all the total trauma of Him Whom God had struck. So He became a dead man; the Dead Man, the Most Holy Dead Man, the Most Innocent Dead Man. He Who was the Life, was dead. Killed by Your abandonment and by our sins.

Darkness becomes deeper. Jerusalem disappears completely. The very slopes of Calvary seem to vanish. Only the top is visible, as if darkness held it high up to receive the only and surviving light, laying it as an offering, with its Divine Trophy, on a pool of liquid onyx, so that it may be seen by love and by hatred.

And from that light which is no longer light, comes the plaintive voice of Jesus: "I am thirsty!" A wind in fact is blowing, which makes even healthy people thirsty — a strong, cold wind that now blows continuously and is full of dust. And I ask myself what pain its violent gusts must have caused to the lungs, the heart, the throat of Jesus and to His frozen, benumbed, wounded limbs. But really, everything has combined forces to torture the Martyr.

A soldier goes towards a jar, in which the assistants of the executioner have put some vinegar with gall, so that with its bitterness it may increase the salivation of those condemned to capital punishment. He takes the sponge immersed in the liquid; he sticks it on a thin yet stiff cane, which is already available nearby and offers the sponge to the dying Victim.

Jesus leans eagerly forward towards the approaching sponge. He looks like a starving baby seeking the nipple of its Mother. Mary sees and certainly has such a thought. Leaning on John, says with a moan: "Oh! and I cannot give even one of my tears... Oh! breast of mine, why do you not trickle milk? Oh! God why do You abandon us thus? A miracle for my Son! Who will lift me up so that I may quench His thirst with my blood, since I have no milk?"

Jesus, who has greedily sucked the sour bitter drink, makes a wry face in disgust. Above all, it must act as a corrosive on His wounded split lips.

He withdraws, loses heart, abandons Himself. All the weight of His body falls heavily on his feet and forward. His wounded extremities are the parts that suffer the dreadful pain as they are torn open by the weight of the body that abandons itself. He makes no further movement to alleviate such pain. His body, from His hips upwards, is detached from the cross and It remained like that.

His head hangs forward so heavenly that His neck seems hollowed in three places; at the throat, which is completely sunken; and at both sides of the sternum cleiod-mastoid. He pants more and more and interruptedly and it sounds more like a death rattle. Now and again a painful fit of coughing brings a light rosy foam to His lips. And the intervals between one expiration and the next one are becoming longer and longer. His abdomen is now motionless. Only His thorax still heaves, but laboriously and with difficulty... pulmonary paralysis is increasing more and more.

And fainter and fainter, sounding like a child's wailing, comes the invocation: "Mother!" And the poor wretch whispers: "Yes, darling, I am here." And when His sight becomes misty and makes Him say: "Mother, where are you? I cannot see you anymore. Are you abandoning Me as well?" And they are not even words, but just a murmur that can hardly be heard by her, who with her heart rather than with her ears, receives every sigh of her dying Son. She says: "No, no, Son! I will not abandon You! Listen to me, my dear... Your Mother is here. She is here ... And she only regrets that she cannot come where You are..."

It is heart-rending... John weeps openly. Jesus must hear him weep, but He does not say anything. I think that His impending death makes Him speak as if He were raving and that He does not even know what He says, and unfortunately, He does not even understand His Mother's consolation and His favorite Apostle's love.

Longinus — who is no longer standing at ease with his arms folded across his chest and one leg crossed over the other alternately, is now instead standing stiff at attention, his left hand on his sword, his right held against his side as if he were on the steps of the imperial throne — does not want to be influenced. But his face is affected in the effort of overcoming his emotion and his eyes begin to shine with tears that only his iron discipline can refrain.

The other soldiers, who were playing dice, have stopped and have stood up, putting on the helmets that had served to cast the dice and they are near the little steps dug in the turf (tufa), looking heedful and silent. The others are on duty and cannot move. They look like statues. But some of those who are closer and hear Mary's words, mutter something between their lips and shake their heads.

There is dead silence. Then in utter darkness, the words: "Everything is accomplished!" are clearly heard and His death rattle grows louder and louder, with longer and longer pauses between one rattle and the next one. Time passes in such distressing rhythm. Life comes back when the air is pierced by the harsh breathing of the Dying Victim... Life stops when the painful sound is no longer heard. One suffers hearing it... one suffers not hearing it... One says: "Enough of this suffering!" and then one says: "Oh God! Let it not be His last breath."

All the Maries are weeping, with their heads leaning against the scarp. And their weeping is clearly heard,
because the crowd is now silent again, to listen to the
death rattles of the Dying Master. There is silence again.
Then the supplication pronounced with infinite kind-
ness, with fervent prayer: "Father, into Your hands I
commit My spirit!"

Further silence. Also, the death rattle becomes
fainter. It is just a breath confined to His lips and throat.

Then, there is the last spasm of Jesus. A dreadful
convulsion that seems to tear the body with the three
nails from the cross, rises three times from the feet to
the head, through all the poor tortured nerves; it heaves
the abdomen three times in an abnormal way, then leaves
it after dilating it as if it were upsetting the viscera and
it drops and becomes hollow as if it were empty; it
heaves, swells and contracts the thorax so violently that
the skin sinks between the ribs which stretch appearing
under the skin and re-opening the wounds of the
scourges; it makes the head fall back violently once,
twice, three times, hitting the wood hard; it contracts
all the muscles of the face in a spasm, accentuating the
deviation of the mouth to the right, it opens wide and
dilates the eyelids under which one can see the eye-
balls roll and the sclerotic appear. The body is all bent;
in the last of the three contractions it is a drawn arch,
which vibrates and is dreadful to look at and then a
powerful cry, unimaginable in that exhausted body,
bursts forth rending the air, the "loud cry" mentioned
by the Gospels and the first part of the word "Mother"
...and nothing else.

His head falls on His chest, His body leans forward,
the trembling stops; He breathes no more. He has
breathed His last. Come, Lord Jesus, Come! Come, Lord
Jesus, Come!